THE SMARTERCHARTER POWER CAT GUIDE: CARIBBEAN

Insiders' Tips for Confident Bareboat Cruising

MICHAEL DOMICAN AND DAVID BLACKLOCK

Illustrated by
KIM DOWNING

Contents

Introduction

Over the past several years, starting in 2017, we have had to change the opening of this series of books to encompass hurricanes, more hurricanes, re-building, and the triumphant return of the charter business to the Caribbean.

Then along came Covid-19.

So we're just going to say, we're still here!

The former one-off, unique situations have now become the new normal. Change is the new constant. We'll have to live with it.

But, as we have said before, the Caribbean is filled with people who have dealt with upheaval and drastic change—be it weather, politics, or pandemic—for centuries. They know how to survive.

So, let's start again!

In these pages we answer the most common (and not-so-common) questions we hear from clients, students, and colleagues as they embrace the art and science of operating a modern cruising Power Cat with a crew of family and friends. Included are descriptions of major chartering areas—the British Virgin Islands (BVI) and neighboring jurisdictions—as well as a glance at more far-afield options. We also attempt a general overview of the Caribbean and its many charms.

We make detailed suggestions as to crew development. Preparations prior to charter. Organizing the galley and food provisioning. Questions to ask your charter company.

Frequently, we point the reader to provisioning and dining options in different locations and offer links for safety and assistance providers (Search and Rescue, Coast Guard, and other services).

We offer links to our preferred sources for local information, websites that offer tips and hints rarely seen elsewhere, as well as social media pages we've found useful.

There are detailed descriptions of anchoring, docking, and mooring practices along with clear illustrations by one of the masters of the medium, Kim Downing.

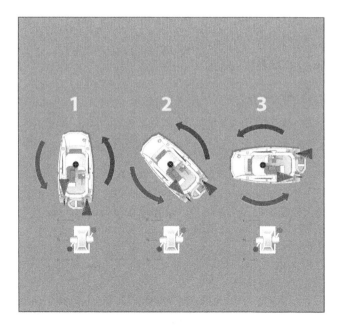

Illustrations by **KIM DOWNING**

We discuss toilets, dinghies, generators, and electrical matters and we try to lighten the tone with the odd joke (*haha!*).

Links to access information useful to the mariner are included in the text, and we include QR codes so the reader can easily access these resources via smartphone or tablet in print editions. In Ch 26, there are links to our website and the information therein, where all the included links can be accessed as well.

NOTE: *We refer frequently to "the Skipper" and define the action aboard ship as being under their direction. All true—but the information is accessible and applicable to any sailor, regardless of experience. On a bareboat charter, the person whose name is on the contract and who is responsible for the well-being and safety of the vessel and occupants undertakes that they, or members of their party, are suitably qualified to operate the vessel. The position of "Skipper" is a role that any suitably experienced person might fill with the consent and presumed supervision of the nominal charterer—for training, practice, or crew development purposes.*

Information and preparation are the keys to happy sailing in any situation.

Welcome Aboard

BACKGROUND

The Caribbean region has long been one of the world's most desirable yacht charter destinations. For sailing yachts, especially, the region features many of the characteristics most important to sailors--consistent wind from the right quarter at the right strength. For the motor yacht, there are other considerations, such as good hotels and restaurants, high quality repair and maintenance facilities, clean fuel, excellent air transport. In addition, the peak time for charter visits—Christmas and New Year—is usually snowbound and chilly in the northern regions of Europe and the Americas. Lately, though, such considerations have been overshadowed by the tragic events of 2017 and after, when hurricanes destroyed the infrastructure on many of the islands and destroyed or damaged hundreds—thousands—of boats and along with them much of the charter industry.

THAT THE INDUSTRY—ALONG with many of the islands—has recovered is to a great extent a testament to the resilience and determination of the Caribbean people. They have had a long acquaintance with adversity—everyone can tell a tale of re-building, of picking up the pieces. But we are in a new era. Things will never be the same again. The events of just a few years ago were seen as a freak event, a rogue season, but they now look increasingly like the new normal.

Those who know and love the region have flocked back to show their support and to honor the determination of the people. And many who had yet to make their first trip to the islands now saw a good reason to go. That respect and appreciation has been returned in ways large and small. Governments are digging deep in their efforts to restore and repair infrastructure. Marinas and hotels are rebuilding. New ventures are being planned and old favorites are being re-imagined and re-built. The mood is upbeat. It's not simply that things will be restored to the way they were, they are being revamped to accommodate the new realities. Charter companies are restocking their fleets—virtually all the major firms have brand-new boats in the water—and adding new options to fit the changing mood of their customers. While everyone keeps a wary eye on the weather map.

THE DISASTERS OF 2017, combined with a changing demographic, have given charter operators an opportunity to configure their fleets more in line with a changed market. Where the customer had most often been an experienced sailor, the new reality encompasses the fact that there is a vast number of boaters who don't care to sail. Time is a luxury. It's all very well to potter along at 5 or 6 knots, but to do so at a high angle of heel—and not always in the desired direction—is too big an ask. A leisurely holiday has to be balanced against the pressures of ever-increasing workloads and the temptations of a dozen other possibilities. And many people "on vacation" find themselves checking into work at some point every day or two.

THE CHARTER COMPANIES found creative ways to accommodate this new reality. First, they extended their sailing fleets to encompass catamarans, which allowed for a greater number of guests in roomy hotel-type accommodation. The boats sailed flat, they were fast, and there's plenty of space to relax. Then the charter companies noticed two things: one was that many of their sailing catamarans returned from charter with the sails obviously never having been used. The other thing they realized was that they were excluding over half of the boating market. Power boaters had fewer options in the charter world—heavy trawler-type boats more suited to long offshore passages than quick runs between islands, or sports fishing boats more suited to a day trip. And there were clearly more power boaters than first realised. But with the introduction of Power Cats, the same comfortable boating experience became available to everybody.

THIS NEW AVAILABILITY OF FAST, comfortable cruising cats helped increase the acceptance of power vessels in the charter environment. Now the beautiful cruising grounds so precious to the sailing community became open to everybody. And many sailors who still enjoyed their passion realized that for the sake of harmony in the family—and to ease their aching bodies—it was just as much fun driving a boat from anchorage to anchorage as it was in sailing the same distance.

First, it was quicker—which meant you could spend longer at the anchorage or visit more destinations in the day's travel. Now the idea of spending five hours leaning at a steep angle and hanging on in a brisk breeze under sail might turn into an hour and a half blasting along on even keels while the family relaxed. Life was good. There was less work to do and more time to snorkel, paddle a kayak, or just read a book. And if you really wanted to sail you could rig up the kite board you brought along and have a blast on that.

MANY SAILORS FELT LIBERATED. As much as they had loved sailing, its pleasures were unreliably dependent upon the fickle ways of Nature. Sometimes, the wind didn't blow—or it blew from the wrong direction or it was too strong, or not strong enough—so they motored around anyway. The joys of being on the water in the sunshine proved to be a large component of their boating pleasure. Just being there was half the fun. Operating the boat was less complicated but still enjoyable. And all their skills in anchoring, docking, and navigating the boat were still as essential as ever.

AND WITH LOTS more engine hours charging the batteries, and with a separate generator pumping out the amps, the kids had Wi-Fi, there was air conditioning, everything worked. Instead of companies offering a mixture of sailing and Power Cats, new companies sprang up devoted solely to the new power yachts. The market became competitive and more inclusive. At the same time, there was increased pressure on the infrastructure—crowded anchorages, larger yachts, more demand for services and amenities. Slowly, of course, the balance is being struck and the vacationing families—and increasingly the flotilla groups—are finding ways to solve the riddle of maximising their pleasure while enjoying the wonders of the region and having a fun boating experience.

FOR MANY, the answer has been the newest category of charter yacht—one that provides comfort and amenities along with speed and exhilaration—the Power Cat.

GETTING STARTED

C hartering a yacht in an unfamiliar location is a bit like renting a car in a foreign country. You know how to drive and you know how to read a map—in fact you have a trusty electronic assistant to help with that part. But it's the other traffic, the unfamiliar signs, the roundabouts, and the over-passes that give you pause.

Do I turn left or right here? Is that a good place to park? What does that sign mean? The gas-oil, is that diesel or petrol? Oops, I mean gas—or do I? As with driving abroad, it's the first day or two that are the most challenging—plus coping with driving on the opposite side of the road, or with a confusing signage system. But by the end of a week, you're charging down the *Autobahn* like you were born to it.

You can read all the books, study up on the regions, talk to friends who have done it before, but once you step aboard a 40-something-foot (13 meter) Power Cat crewed by your family or friends in often lumpy conditions—well, things can seem a bit daunting. Especially when the weather forecast is in an unfamiliar language or dialect, delivered via a crackling radio.

We're here to help. We've spent years in the Caribbean and know that our experience could be of benefit. We aim to share our knowledge and a few tricks we've picked up about the region and its inhabitants—and to have you confidently guiding a modern Power Cat around some of the most beautiful and accessible cruising grounds the world has to offer.

Now, bareboating Caribbean style doesn't have to mean casually cruising with a Red Stripe in one hand while the autopilot takes you...somewhere. Rather, it means piloting a well-appointed yacht in close-to-ideal conditions without the issues that often plague higher latitude sailors—unpredictable weather, chilly temperatures, foul weather gear, fog, big tidal ranges, and strong currents—or windy days better suited to kiting than boating. At least not all the time.

Power Cats in the world's charter fleets have become stunningly sophisticated in recent years. They boast comfort, style, and more intricate systems. Virtually every model comes standard with a high capacity generator, air conditioning, electric freshwater heads/toilets, sound systems with speakers in multiple locations, and a reliable Wi-Fi connection. Larger models generally boast a water-maker and other amenities.

This sophistication brings with it a greater convenience but it can also bring greater complication and confusion. Electrical systems can always misbehave, generators can quit in the middle of the night.

Murphy's great law prevails: If it can, it will. Break down, that is. (Though hopefully not on your vacation!).

Fortunately, along with the sophistication of the Power Cats there has been a related improvement in customer service—help is but a (free) phone call away.

BOAT OPERATION IS AS MUCH an art as a science. But there is rarely just one correct way to do anything on a boat, bareboat or otherwise. Whether it be docking, anchoring, battling head winds and swells or running before a storm, there is almost always more than one way of pulling it off. So, if you have a technique that works and that won't break or scratch anything—or raise your blood pressure (or that of anyone around you)—stay with it. But we hope our guide will add to your body of knowledge and perhaps offer a fresh perspective on some of the familiar aspects of the Skipper's skill set.

Research and planning are key to any successful voyage. One excellent source for information on the Caribbean is the message board Traveltalkonline.com . If you're new to the area you wish to charter, go on this site a few weeks or months prior and ask questions—you'll get some relevant information from fellow charterers or year-round residents.

Another good source is Noonsite.com which has extensive information on the cruising grounds of the Caribbean—and the rest of the world, too. It is specially useful for information on Customs and Immigration requirements. In addition, many of the specific islands have related Facebook groups for cruisers and visitors which are worth exploring.

There are, of course, many apps for phone and tablet that cover the Caribbean. The ActiveCaptain app is one we like, particularly if your charter yacht has a Garmin chartplotter or Navionics e-charts.

On reliable standby is the Simon and Nancy Scott Cruising Guide to the Virgin Islands, (cruisingguides.com), the classic reference. Many charter companies supply a copy of that book, or the Doyle Cruising Guide for the region you'll be in. This excellent, long-established publication has a useful website with links to many amenities, such as a list of Facebook groups for just about every island in the region. doyleguides.com

NOTE: *The individual charter company web sites have a wealth of information for the destinations they serve. By scanning them all you can get a comprehensive idea of the options and attractions available throughout the Caribbean.*

3

THE CHARTER BUSINESS
FUN IN THE SUN

P ower Cats have quickly gained significant market share in the Caribbean. Charter companies, long accustomed to a sailing clientele who offer proof of competence by way of certificates and log books, have had to find ways to evaluate their new customers. Does the skipper have experience of more than a day trip? Some charter companies are stricter than others—a trait that favors the consumer, in that the stricter companies tend to have the less-abused and better-maintained (and often the newest) boats. Most require a comprehensive resume for the designated skipper and, on larger boats, at least one other member of the party.

Company staff will often drive the boat off the dock at the beginning, and back on to the dock for you at the end of the charter. It's just easier and more efficient that way. The base managers realize that a forty-something-foot long, twenty-foot wide boat is likely the biggest moving vehicle many charter guests have ever handled so they want to make it easy for you. And with the rebuilding of docks and marinas, there can be boats tied up all over the place—you'll have enough to worry about without having to navigate your way through a parking lot. And the company employee can demonstrate some of the tricks of their trade on the way.

The main differences among the charter grounds of the Caribbean lie in the convenience of travel, ease of shopping, and the distances that have to be covered when getting from one anchorage to the other. It's no surprise that the busiest charter grounds in the region —the British Virgin Islands—are a short distance from mainland USA, deal in US dollars as their official currency, speak English, and are very stable politically.

Not only that, they are laid out in such a way that a chain of small islands on the south-eastern edge provides protection from waves from that quarter, while the larger islands provide a great degree of shelter from the storm-generated swells emanating off the North Atlantic. The resulting relative calm in the main channel of the chain, the Sir Francis Drake Channel, explains its colloquial name, *Drake Lake*.

RECENT DEVELOPMENTS ANNOUNCED by major charter companies suggest new Power Cat cruising grounds are opening up. The Moorings has Power Cats on offer in six Caribbean destinations. Currently, Dream Yacht Charters has availability in a couple of destinations, while the biggest powercat-only player in the Caribbean is the relatively new entrant MarineMax Vacations in the BVI with a modern fleet of purpose-built charter vessels.

Airports are expanding, too, as islands compete more fiercely for the tourist and leisure traveler. And even without airport construction and expansion, new participants continue to join the market.

Currently there are direct flights from New York, Miami, and other US and Canadian cities to over a dozen destinations all over the Caribbean. Much of this development has been spurred by the recent catastrophic weather events. It makes sense to spread the risk as widely as possible so if one charter base or airport is knocked out, there will be another waiting to receive guests.

To the east of the BVI, the cruising grounds of St. Martin/Sint Maarten lie exposed to the swells rolling in from the North Atlantic and Africa. Farther south, the Grenadines and other islands present some challenges in the distances a boat has to cover to get from one anchorage to another—though those difficulties are offset by the relative lack of other cruisers, making these islands almost at times a private playground. In these more exposed waters, you're going to be less likely to use your Power Cat's maximum cruising speed when dealing with wind and waves.

Where sailors begin their Caribbean chartering adventures is purely a matter of choice and convenience. Many cruisers began chartering in the soft waters of the BVI before venturing further down the Antilles chain. The options available will suit every preference— some destinations have direct flights from Europe and the US, others are a bit harder to reach—while the charter becomes a little more challenging. As you venture east and south, cruisers are obliged to fend for themselves to a greater degree—which is not necessarily a bad thing.

Most of the charter companies cited above also have bases further down the islands. St. Vincent, Grenada, Guadeloupe, Martinique, Antigua and Barbuda, St Martin and its neighboring islands—as well as those destinations already mentioned—are well served by the major companies and some local ones as well. These destinations are, in the main, well served by air transport, too—either directly or with one stop along the way. While not every destination is serviced by a Power Cat operator, it's always wise to ask since the companies are constantly experimenting with customer demand and vessel availability.

THE CARIBBEAN IS A BOATING PLAYGROUND, able to indulge all manner of bareboating adventurers with options fitting every level of expertise and experience. So when choosing a charter company it pays to learn whether they offer discounts for future charters and other inducements, loyalty programs and the like. You can also negotiate for better prices at different times—or if no shift on the pricing, the company might offer you an extra day or a night's pre-boarding or a free kayak.

Starting your charter on a Wednesday and finishing on a Tuesday might be worth a good amount of change. It's always worth trying, though the newest boats are usually in solid demand and not subject to discount. Ask where the best deals might be—maybe one of the other islands is doing less business than projected and is priced accordingly.

On the other hand, it might be in your interest to pay a little extra to cement a relationship with a top charter company. As competition increases, incentives will surely follow—and loyalty be rewarded.

A YACHT IS an expensive asset to own. Anyone who lives near a marina will have noticed that boats seem to sit in their slips for most of the year—going nowhere and doing nothing.

As yacht ownership has diminished over the past decade or more, the yacht charter business has increased exponentially. Why own a yacht when you can rent one for a week or two in different parts of the world? Or, why not own a yacht that allows you to sail a similar model in different parts of the world whilst yours is earning you an income? And even if you do own a boat in your home waters, it will be expensive and a lot of wear and tear for you to have it delivered to the Caribbean.

This change in boating habits has been one of the drivers behind the rapid innovations in yacht construction and design—which in turn have made the charter yacht the attractive option it has become. But while changes are inevitable, the charter business is, and should long remain, a strong pillar of local economies. Each year the boats get more comfortable, the amenities more varied, access more efficient, destinations more welcoming. The great secret of yacht charter is that it has many price points from the top tier to the relatively barebones, but once you're on the water the fun is the same and the experience, well, priceless.

We look forward to seeing you out there!

4

PREP TALK

GETTING READY

W hether this is your first charter or just the most recent, there are always new elements to consider. If it's a purely family trip, the needs and preferences of all the participants will be fairly well established. There may be an allergy to manage, a medical condition to treat, an athletic routine that puts conditions on the charter. Does someone need to run for an hour every day? Do yoga? Some of these requirements might narrow the list of destinations available to the group.

Has everyone been on a boat trip before? Is this the first trip to a particular part of the world, or a specific area of the Caribbean? Give everyone ample time to research the destination—Or if the destination hasn't been finalized, let them research the options.

If you can manage it, try to be on charter around the time of Full Moon. Many areas celebrate the moon with dance parties and *jump-ups*. This involves research—tides, weather—as well as chart work and close reading of the cruising guides. And, unless you are a fan of sailing regattas, you might want to avoid Antigua during Race Week, the BVI during the Spring Regatta, Sint Maarten during the

Heineken Regatta—which all follow one another pretty closely at the beginning of Spring. The waterways are busy!

NOTE: *Given present conditions, health protocols may put a damper on these long-established events—but not for long (we hope).*

Before coming on charter, there are some essential tasks that need to be tackled. Now is a great opportunity to develop crew cohesion. The Skipper—and there may be more than one, of course, perhaps sharing the responsibility—can ask different members of the party to do research, to practice techniques, to get themselves into the adventure mindset. If you are partial to Facebook, WhatsApp, Instagram, or other social media platforms, you could set up a private group for all participants. Or just a simple email group will suffice. That way people can share photos, web sites, articles, instructional videos and other relevant information. And get the family and friends thinking about the part they will play in the day-to-day operation of the yacht.

CREW ASSIGNMENTS: Here are some ways to involve your crew in the pre-charter prep:

- Most Important—practice your knots! Like every boat afloat, the Power Cat relies on rope, or lines, to tie it up and to tie things down. The #1 most-neglected aspect of power boat operation is the mastery of these basic knots—the Reef Knot/Square Knot, Bowline, Clove Hitch, Cleat Hitch, Round Turn and Two Half Hitches, Figure 8/Stopper Knot, Sheet Bend, Cow Hitch, and Rolling Hitch. Download here
- You'll need these knots to attach mooring lines, brace the dinghy, secure paddle boards and dive tanks. To tie up to a dock. To attach fenders to a railing. Consider having a

knot-tying session weeks before the charter so everyone can practise—make a game of it! It's a safety issue—you want to be able to rely upon your fellow sailors to be able to secure a knot without too much hesitation.

- Create simple Passage Plans for each day's journey (with options for those days when you decide to do nothing but loll on the beach or snorkel the reefs). These can be done way ahead of time and can be multiple choice. That is, make rudimentary passage plans with options should there be a large swell or intense wind gusts. Basically, do you turn left or right as you leave the anchorage? And if conditions change during the day, do you have an alternative? It's all very well to improvise when the destinations are just 15 minutes apart, but in areas where you have to motor for an hour or more, it's good to have a plan. Download a sample at: https://tinyurl.com/6tya9tfv (as part of a bigger Safety Pack)

- Pay attention to swell forecasts, making allowances for wave events when large waves emanating from distant North Atlantic storms arrive in the islands—much to the joy of surfers but the bane of sailors who failed to check the forecast. They may wake in the early morning to find a normally quiet anchorage now exposed to these incoming rollers.

- Also, when making passage plans, be modest about your daily mileage at least in the beginning. An hour on the water can be more than enough for tender stomachs after a long flight. Maybe try a quick jaunt to a nearby beach for a swim and lunch before heading to your first overnight destination. Though be prepared to stay at your first anchorage, especially if you have young kids aboard.

- Contact the charter company to learn what brand of chartplotter your powercat is equipped with. There will likely be an app that you can download to your smart device and link directly to it. Most companies have a chat bot or inquiry line for such queries. (And see below for further questions you might want to ask.)

- Assign positions to your crew based on their expertise and experience—helmsman, navigator—and let them do their research. Younger crew can perform wonders as lookouts, fender monitors, water-toy wranglers and the like.
- Suggest reading material for your crew—guidebooks, charts, online discussion boards.

DELEGATE CREW TO GATHER INFORMATION:

Check the charter company web site to confirm what items are included on the boat and what are optional extras—toys (such as Stand Up Paddleboards), floating toys (inflatable flamingos), Wi-Fi, safety netting (for young children), hammocks and the like. If the information is not available, send an email. If possible, get a contact name at the base you are going to for on-the-ground information. Check the web forums such as traveltalkonline.com. (https://www.tinyurl.com/4k2yccc4) People there can help with personal contact details for helpful staff members.

Ask the charter company for provisioning information, such as which companies deliver to the boat. Look on the online discussion groups, as well, for references and preferences.

Request an inventory list by way of towels, soap/shampoo and galley cleaning items, garbage bags and insect spray. Some charter operators provide a starter pack to cover you for the first couple of days, others don't provide anything in that department at all.

While the charter company will provide a cruising guide on the boat, it's a good idea to have a copy ahead of time to help with the planning. It's a great way to keep a record of your trip, too. You can ask the charter company if they'll send you a copy (some do) or else get one from Bluewater Books, Amazon, or your local bookstore.

Explore options for rendezvous dives or lessons, eco-tours and other high-demand frolics. Be cautious about making commitments far in advance, since weather and other factors might dictate last-minute itinerary changes that make it difficult to keep appointments. Aside from Thanksgiving and Christmas/New Year, you can most often book a dive or other activity when you arrive for your charter—or the week prior to your arrival—and are better able to make an informed decision on weather and itinerary.

BROWSE WEB SITES TO see what events might be upcoming at your destination—Full Moon parties, national holidays, Mardi Gras, Carnival, New Year's. French islands have their special days, as do the Dutch, British, and US territories.

PERSONAL EQUIPMENT:

Consider your clothing options: people often bring far too much. T-shirts (or equivalent), shorts, and sandals or flip-flops are the general rule though you might want to dress a bit for a night out. You can always bolster your supply of beachwear at many of the bars, restaurants, and boutiques along the way. One complication is that if you leave home in winter, you'll need warm clothing for the beginning and ending segments—which you may be able to leave at the charter base rather than bring onboard. Also, the seating position on the Power Cat is quite high above the water and there may not be a lot of shelter, so bring something warm and waterproof to wear when underway. The boats often have wrap-around Eisenglass curtains which may have to be rolled up to survive a blustery day's breeze or a high-speed run.

- Bring rash guards and swimming tops (for protection

against sun, and stings and scrapes when around coral), snorkels and masks that fit properly (kid-sized ones particularly) though the boat will come equipped with a variety of sizes. If you are chartering in the winter season, prepare for some (relatively) chilly evenings. And everyone should have a wide-brimmed hat with a lanyard for sun protection.

- Luggage is a sensitive issue. Storage is at a minimum aboard the boat though you might be able to store empty suitcases—or ones stuffed with your winter gear—at the charter base while you are on the water. Soft luggage like a duffel bag is preferred for the boat since it can be rolled up and stowed under the bunk. Also, the farther afield you go—and the more flights you have to take—the more likely that a bag could go missing, so pack as lightly as possible.

- Check with your doctor for all your medications—you may need to renew prescriptions. Bring medications in their original containers and have copies of all prescriptions—particularly of unusual medications—since authorities have been known to request them.

- Bring seasickness remedies. Scopolamine trans-dermal patches are highly effective (but not for everyone).

- Make sure all documents are up to date—passports, driving licenses, boating resume/certifications, etc. Do you need visas? Let your credit card company know your plans—even if they say you don't have to--since the Caribbean is a bit of a trigger for the banks. They may send a verification text or a phone call that you are unable to access, requesting a response before they release funds.

- See if your phone plan includes the country you'll be in—otherwise roaming will suck up money. Ask to have it added and make sure it covers data as well as voice calls! And get the details on any Wi-Fi service the charter company provides.

Gear to Bring:

- Hand-held VHF radio. These days, almost all the islands have reliable mobile service and most smartphones work here, so many sailors use an app like WhatsApp as a messaging system. But as a safety measure and as backup, bring a handheld VHF if you have one. They work well should the Cellular network go down. All the better if yours has a GPS built in.
- Hand-held GPS, with spare batteries or charger, likewise. For when the main chart plotter goes down (in an electrical storm for instance). You may not need it—but when you do, you really do. Mobile devices generally have a GPS capability—but make sure yours can work independently of Internet hookup.
- Some short (10 foot) length of thin but strong (Spectra, if possible) line. Your bareboat won't have many spare short lengths of strong line, which is handy for a multitude of jobs from securing the dinghy fuel tank to keeping the Stand Up Paddleboard (SUP) attached to the boat. Leave it behind when you finish charter.
- Cable ties in assorted colors to mark the anchor chain and other items. The needn't be very long--medium sized, or differing sizes. They can be useful for many purposes.
- LED headlamp for BBQ duty, night-time anchor inspection (with a red-light option), dinghy operation, and a host of other uses, such as reading in the cockpit at night.
- Pack your own basic first-aid kit with anti-bacterial cream, your preferred pain relievers, sun cream (SPF 30 is sufficient--but make sure it is reef-safe), top-level sticking plasters (Band-Aid type), and any other favorite brands. Most places in the Caribbean carry US brands along with French, Dutch, and British—depending on where you are.
- Bring a selection of multi-sized zip-lock style bags. They are good for bagging sunscreen, toothpaste, meal leftovers and other messy stuff as well as wet items such as bathing

suits; and documents, electronics, and other sensitive items. Wash them and take them home with you.

- A good underwater camera—because you can't take your phone everywhere.
- Hammock (the netting type, without crossbars) plus attaching straps to rig between support structures on the boat's hardtop or transversely across the stern area. Some smaller ones can be rigged in the cockpit area for storing fruit such as oranges and bananas and/or dive masks, etc. And you can tie it between palm trees ashore (just watch out for the falling coconuts!)
- Insulated drinking water bottles. The islands have become very conscious of the environmental costs of plastic. (Some charters now appoint a recyclables officer to monitor plastic bags etc. These look like jelly fish in the water and can be fatal to turtles).
- Sharpie-style marker pens and masking tape to mark items such as water bottles, can and bottle tops for quick identification in a fridge or cooler.
- Also bring white electrical tape *not duct tape* to mark switches controlling dinghy lifts, anchor windlass and other items.
- Notebook (for chart briefing, boat briefing, etc.)
- *Speedo*-type swim goggles for use when operating the boat or the dinghy during rain squalls. Ski goggles (mask-type) will work even better. These are good because the nose is free—unlike with a dive mask where the nose is encapsulated in the body of the mask and creates fog.
- Mini flashlights.
- Dry Bag: if you want to go ashore by paddle board—or swim to that famous bar that won't let you dinghy over.

MONEY MATTERS:

Bring plenty of cash. Many of the islands have inefficient communications, even at the best of times—making credit card payments unreliable. Phone connections can go down, internet traffic can be awfully slow. In addition, banks may charge extra fees for the Caribbean, making it expensive for the business owner, so they insist on a high minimum amount for credit card charges or impose a fee for the service. Cash is king. In many places the US dollar is easily accepted, even in Euro areas.

PERSONAL ITEMS

All the following should fit into a single soft duffel-type bag.

First question: Shoes/ no shoes?

Answer: It depends. Many sailors prefer to go barefoot on the boat. Which is fine until you stub a toe on a deck fitting or slip on a wet cabin sole. If you do choose to wear shoes onboard, they must have a light-colored sole. White is good. They needn't be fancy $100 nautical jobs—grab a $20 pair from the Big Box store or the super-market. They only need to last a week—leave them behind for the dock guys. Never wear them off the boat—they'll just bring sand and dirt aboard. A slip-on type rather than a lace-up is best. So long as they have a decent grip they'll do. Off the boat you'll be wearing flip-flops. If you prefer to wear shoes, bring a second pair for shore-side. And Crocs are always an option.

Mostly, you'll be living in shorts and t-shirts or your swimsuit. If you're short of an item there are plenty of shops eager to sell you a shirt, shorts, hat, whatever. Bring the basics:

- 2-3 pairs of decent quick-dry shorts.
- 1 pair of long pants/dress skirt (if you intend to go to a more upscale restaurant).
- 1 dress shirt with collar (ditto)
- 1 T-shirt/top per day (buy any extras at the many bars and restaurants)
- 2 shirts (with long sleeves preferably. Quick-dry, SPF-30 and above). For sailing and general outdoors work.

- 6-8 pair underpants (you won't need to wash them, and they take up no space. Pack them up in a plastic bag and take them home).
- 2 swim suits
- 1 sweater or vest/cardigan (for cool evenings)
- 1 lightweight waterproof jacket—preferably GoreTex
- At least one pair polarized sunglasses (plus safety/retainer cord)
- 1 good protective hat
- Medications (bring a copy of any prescriptions). Plus any favorite teas, music, books, games, etc.

NOTE: *If you are taking multiple flights, pack a carry-on bag with a change of clothes (T-shirt and shorts plus hoodie), swimsuit, and toiletry items, etc. for a couple of days. Also pack relevant medications—along with copies of their prescriptions. The more changes you make en route the greater the likelihood your luggage will not arrive at the same time as you.*

5

PROVISIONING

ORDER IN

No matter which island destination you choose, or which charter company, your arrival at the charter base can often turn into a confusion of conflicting priorities and last-minute adjustments.

Not only will you be exhausted from the travel, but there will be briefings to attend, supplies to purchase and stow, crew to instruct—amongst other things. One time-saver is to ask your charter company about pre-ordering provisions. Many of the islands have supermarkets or specialist vendors that offer this service—or the charter company might do it in-house.

ALTHOUGH IT MIGHT SEEM tempting to simply pre-order everything and have it available when you arrive—what happens if your flight is delayed or your boat isn't ready? Do you really want your pricey perishable items sitting in the hot sun for hours? (Some charter companies do have refrigerated storage available for deliveries, so ask.)

Hold off on the perishables, but do get your packaged, canned, and bottled items—especially water—delivered. Having the heavy stuff dropped off leaves you free to shop around for meat, seafood, fruit, vegetables, cheeses, and other delicate items. Your charter company should be able to provide links to local stores that'll deliver direct to your boat. And most larger islands can accommodate diets of the gluten-free or vegan variety these days. Most large supermarkets will have a taxi-driver waiting outside for customers to bring you back—or the taxi that brought you from the charter base will arrange to come back in 45 minutes or so (but do get the driver's name and phone number!)

The taxi drivers know the drill. They'll drop you off and set a time to pick you up. *Get their phone number!*

It's tempting to think of finding wonderful fresh produce and fruit picked just days before on an island farm but it's hardly ever going to happen. Most provisions come in big containers from Miami twice a week. The French islands seem to have delicacies flown in on the last flight from Paris every day...but that might just be a fantasy! (Although many of the French islands will provide you with fresh baguettes twice a day.) Ask your charter company if there are any local fresh food growers or markets. The BVI's Aragorn Dick-Read supplies organically grown local herbs and veges and can deliver by arrangement (goodmoonfarm.com).

It helps to have a good idea of what you'll need for the duration of the trip. Charter chef Deb Mahan gave us these tips:

- Create a basic spreadsheet with a menu plan for each day. Working from that, you can be precise about the amount of vegetables, starches, and proteins that you will need.
- Count how many chicken breasts, how many rashers of bacon, the number of eggs and so on.
- As storage space is limited and refrigeration not always reliable, plan to eat the more perishable items earlier in the charter.
- Start your shopping list with items required for the first meal of the day through to dinners. As you think of an item, group it into proteins, fruit and vegetables, dry goods, and grocery items. You can then pick out non-perishable items that you can pre-order ahead of arrival, making your personal shopping much easier.
- Plan your itinerary to include a stop with a supermarket or decent grocery halfway through your trip.
- Have a meal ashore at a recommended restaurant every second day or so to give the chefs a break—and to make the provisions last a bit longer. And because you're on vacation!
- Follow this link for Deb's Basic Meal Plan spreadsheet tinyurl.com/tvoos6x
- And ask about genuine local producers for a taste of fresh locally grown fruit and vegetables. In several Caribbean islands there are farmers and purveyors of indigenous fruit and veg.We have assembled a number of links to purveyors and provisioning stores throughout the Caribbean. Access all these links at tinyurl.com/4m6263nm
- Some destinations will permit you to bring special foods such as frozen meats or seafood with you, packed in dry ice or just stacked while frozen inside a good travel cooler, such as a Yeti. Check with your airline!
- Water toys and other items such as Stand Up Paddleboards (SUPs), kayaks, noodles, can be ordered through your charter company and their partners.

6

KIDS ON BOARD

Power Cat design has changed in recent years. Once a PC might have been a slightly modified catamaran hull, minus the mast but with bigger engines. Now they are designed and built for purpose, with a number of innovative features not found on sailing catamarans or monohull powerboats.

The wide-open interior spaces and deck areas of the Power Cat offer challenges for young children, so take extra care in both choosing the boat and in operating the one you've chosen. All boats will slam into an oncoming wave or lurch down the back of one that's just passed, leaving the little ones sliding about--if they aren't properly supervised. Catamarans will bounce around quickly and, because of their greater speed potential, can throw crew in unexpected directions. And an oncoming swell (or a large wake) can stop them quickly too!

If you have small children on board, ask the charter company to attach netting around the perimeter of the boat. Most will do so for a small extra fee—but the cost is nothing compared to the peace of mind it can induce.

Regardless of age, you must have life jackets (PFDs) that fit your children. Ask ahead of your arrival and check that they are aboard when you get there. For kids under 6, some charter companies recommend bringing theirs along if you have one.

Do the same with dive masks: if the kids have one at home, pack it in the luggage—that way they won't have to endure an oversized leaky mask. During high season, choice may be restricted at the charter base. If your kids are small, bring small swim fins too, if you have them at home. These are items that not all charter companies are able to provide—though they might have partners who can supply them to you if needed.

OLDER KIDS (OVER 10, say) like to get involved in the operation of the boat. There are many things they can do—sort out swim fins and masks, check that SUPs and kayaks are firmly attached to the railings, monitor the dinghy in its davits or being towed, and even operate it if they fit the criteria laid down by the charter company. They can even sweep out the saloon and help with garbage and other tasks that are essential everyday, such as clearing laundry off the railings prior to getting underway and looking for loose items that might blow away. Give the older kids the responsibility for checking bilges, emptying holding tanks and generally making themselves useful. And they make great lookouts!

One way to do it is to create a schedule and break the kids into teams so they can alternate duties. Teams can be assigned deck duty (tidying up loose items, securing SUPs, etc.), saloon duty (washing dishes, putting things away that might fly around the saloon when underway, tidying up toys and card games, separating recyclables etc.) plumbing duty (checking bilge float switches are clear of obstruction, prepping the holding tanks for emptying when underway in open water, etc.) and any other daily tasks that need attending.

KIDS LOVE to learn new stuff. BVI charter captain and instructor Donna Smith Acquaro, says, "I recommend encouraging children to learn along the way. Bring books with the flora and fauna of the area--you can often find them at the charter base. Also, drawing materials and shock- and water-proof cameras."

And look at what your charter company (or local third-party vendor) offers in the way of water toys. These are age-dependent but range from swim noodles to kayaks and SUPs. Also take a look at your local drugstore or mall outlets—they often have kid-sized inflatable toys and the like at ridiculous prices. Many folks bring these toys and leave them on the boat when they're done.

PARENTS often bemoan the fact that kids on a boat seem to want to spend time texting on their phones or watching Harry Potter on an iPad, rather than enjoying the gorgeous azure waters. But we have found that it pays to indulge the young set initially. The boat is an unfamiliar environment—often much friendlier to adult preferences than youthful ones. In a day or two the kids ought to relax and adapt. If not, it's easy to distract them with trips ashore. In most island destinations there are often stops along the way with kid-friendly food and sand beneath the feet.

A little family hiking trip can change the atmosphere immediately. Some restaurants offer kid-friendly entertainment, such as pirate shows and sing-alongs and for older kids there are surf clinics and kiteboard lessons. Ask at your orientation/chart briefing if they recommend any child-oriented shore stops.

Some island beaches feature amenities such as inflatable climbing walls, safe and easy snorkeling areas, even sandpits and playpens— aka the beach. Older kids (parents too) might enjoy hiking to the top of the island on dedicated trails to take in the view. Some areas feature horse and pony riding and other activities to suit various ages.

IF ALL ELSE FAILS, you'll at least have the onboard Wi-Fi to conjure up some silly videos—just don't check the news

7

THE CHART BRIEFING

This briefing is an essential element of the bareboat charter. While it is very rarely brief and it's not merely about the chart, it is crucial that the skipper and at least one other crew member attend. If time permits, and the crew are interested, bring them all.

NOTE: *In this time of contagion, charter companies might restrict the briefing to just one crew member and insist upon some form of Social Distancing. It may even be offered online via a YouTube video.*

Most charter companies offer a group briefing for all outgoing charters, either in the early evening the day prior to charter, or the morning of the first day—often both. You'll learn about the area and the environment in detail, as well as current events both cultural and meteorological. It can be overwhelming, so be sure to take notes for later reference.

This is an important resource even if you've sailed in the area before —things change all the time and memory is not a reliable navigational instrument! If some of your crew arrive late, have them sit-in on the next available briefing. That way you'll all be on the same page.

NOTE: *Memory is not a reliable navigational instrument. Take notes.*

If you hope to get out of the base quickly, the remaining crew could be going through the ship's inventory, stowing provisions, doing any last-minute shopping or sorting swim fins, topping off water tanks and all the other sundry tasks that remain undone. The following are among the topics covered in the chart briefing—and be sure to ask if something you are concerned about isn't specifically addressed:

- How to get a local weather forecast and where to get updates via VHF or local radio each morning or evening.
- Swell warnings and projected weather events.
- Any recent biohazards that have been reported (jellyfish during summer months, fly outbreaks, Sargassum seaweed beachings).
- Local dos and don'ts—dress codes, for instance. Some islands encourage a modest presentation.
- Current events that can impact your trip—you can encounter powerboat Poker Runs at various times of the year. These might affect your ability to anchor or find a mooring at a favored destination on a particular day. And they often take over the fuel docks for hours, so you aren't able to replenish diesel and water. Also there are various Full Moon parties and such that may require finding a mooring much earlier in the day than normal.
- A sample itinerary with the most popular stops described— as well as the No-Go areas, where your insurance coverage might be void.

- Communications protocols, such as phone numbers for assistance, etc.

- Procedures to follow on return from charter, such as fueling requirements.
- Hazards and/or local warnings—anything from a sunk boat or an exclusionary zone, to possible crime situations (in some locations, not all) such as dinghy theft hot spots.
- The types of Navigational Markers you'll encounter—such as Cardinal Buoys—and any missing markers, as well. Plus any special rules, off-limit areas, etc.
- Spring in the Caribbean is the time for high-level racing regattas—you can find yourself suddenly in the middle of a hard-charging fleet. Check with your briefer.
- At almost any time of the year, there are sailing club flotillas and other groups that, while fun to share a dance floor with ashore, can make finding a mooring somewhat challenging. Such groups won't all be leaving from the same charter base as you of course, so ask around.
- Try to obtain an itinerary from any such flotilla—just walk up to one of the participating boats on your dock (you'll know by the flags and banners flying from the topping lift) and ask. Customer Service personnel at the charter company should have an itinerary sheet at their disposal, too. Some areas are host to regattas put on by the sailing magazines and yacht clubs.
- So if you encounter any such group, try to get their itinerary—and either follow along or go the opposite direction!
- You can also ask the personnel on a crewed yacht if they know any information that could assist you. Usually they are only too happy to advise—they'd rather help out before you start the charter than have to come to the rescue when boats drag anchor at midnight in an unruly and crowded anchorage!
- Make a record of any changes to relevant phone numbers for things like medical clinics, emergency services, hospitals and the like. (These are generally listed in the onboard Briefing Manual, but the information may need updating.)

- The information you learn at the Chart Briefing can impact the final version of your Passage Plan. So make sure you review any plans already written out.
- You may have written passage plans weeks before you arrive in the islands. If not, research tide heights and times, phases of the moon, particular events at different destinations. Write up a number of alternate plans and, depending on the weather patterns on the day of charter, you can choose which one to implement.

NOTE: *Tides have minimal effect in the Caribbean, but the resulting currents can affect entrances and narrow channels.*

ABOUT THOSE SWELLS:

From late October until late May, exactly corresponding to the busiest charter season, Caribbean islands can be subject to sudden changes to the near-shore sea state. These sudden changes have nothing to do with the local atmospheric conditions.

The ambient weather could be perfectly fine with sunny skies and moderate trade winds from the east to north-east with the usual wind-driven swells of around 3-4 feet (around one meter)—all perfectly normal in the West Indies. But two thousand miles away in the North Atlantic, autumnal and winter storms kick up big seas that, 2-3 days later, ripple their way south to the islands' warm and sunny shores.

Along the way, these large waves diminish in height and, because they're not all moving at exactly the same speed, catch up and merge with one another to form rows of fewer but more powerful waves. If you're flying down from the north-east part of North America on your way to the Caribbean you sometimes see them clearly if you're in a window seat.

In the ocean, this accumulated power is not manifest as higher waves but as longer-period waves: that is the time between each successive crest or trough of a wave gets longer, often around twice what the period was before they merged. When you leave coastal waters and sail truly offshore — blue water sailing — this is one of the big differences sailors notice, these longer period swells caused by distant storms.

The reason the coastal sailor doesn't usually experience this is that waves slow down as they encounter shallower water and they start to bunch-up to one another and get taller—often twice their deep water height. This effect of the seabed on the incoming waves creates what are known as 'ground swells' or 'ground seas'. Be forewarned: the reason surfers flock to them is the very reason sailors should avoid them.

FOR CENTURIES, bays and harbors with good holding ground that offer some shelter from this E/NE quarter have provided safe overnight shelter for vessels. Whatever modest wave action is occurring outside the bay is blocked by a protruding headland or semi-exposed reef that reflects or absorbs the waves' energy.

But when the waves come from a direction different to the local wind—from the direction of those distant storms—these normally safe bays are left exposed and become uncomfortable and sometimes even dangerous to be in.

The best way to avoid them is to check not just the wind forecast and whether it's going to rain or not but to look at the wave forecast as well—and not just for the day ahead but especially for the evening ahead.

All the online forecast sites offer this and the dedicated surfer sites do an especially good job. But what you need to look out for are overnight changes to both the wave direction and its period.

Virgin Islands, British - British Virgin Islands ★	☀ 06:48 - 17:44	☾ 17

GFS 27 km	ⓘ Info	⊞ Forecast	⩗ Graph	⩶ 2D	⠿ More

Init: 22.12.2018 06 UTC	Sa 05h	Sa 08h	Sa 11h	Sa 14h	Sa 17h	Sa 20h	Su 05h	Su 08h	Su 11h	Su 14h	Su 17h	Su 20h	Mo 05h	Mo 08h	Mo 11h	Mo 14h
Wind speed (knots)	14	14	15	16	16	15	13	14	13	14	13	15	15	16	17	15
Wind gusts (knots)	16	16	17	18	18	17	14	16	15	15	15	17	17	17	19	17
Wind direction	←	←	←	←	←	←	↙	←	←	←	←	↙	↙	←	←	←
Wave (m)	0.9	0.9	0.9	1	1	0.9	0.8	0.8	0.8	0.8	0.8	0.9	0.9	1	1	1
Wave period (s)	10	10	10	6	7	7	8	8	8	14	13	12	10	6	6	6
Wave direction	↓	↓	↓	↙	↙	↙	↙	↙	↙	↓	↓	↓	↓	↙	←	←
*Temperature (°C)	26	26	27	27	27	26	26	26	26	27	26	26	26	26	26	26

A typical forecast showing changing swell direction

WHEN WAVES SHIFT (if only for a few hours) to the NW or N do not plan to overnight in north-facing bays. In fact, get away from north-facing coasts and seek shelter on the south sides of islands where at all possible (and in the Caribbean with so many islands to choose from, it's almost always possible). Call the charter company for advice if you're unsure. They know the islands and have access to all the local forecasts so they can either reassure you of your choice or give you a pointer to somewhere safer.

WHAT ARE the likely risks when stuck in a vulnerable anchorage after sunset?

Unless you're the boat's owner and experienced in piloting a boat in the dark off an unfamiliar, poorly lighted coast you're simply begging for trouble. Even then, should any accidental damage happen to your boat—or anything you hit—your insurance would be void because charter yachts are forbidden from being under way at night unless they have an explicit, written waiver from the charter company.

Going ashore in the dinghy in these conditions is out of the question: if it didn't get swamped during an attempted beach landing, it would get swamped trying to get back out. Provided, that is, the dinghy survived being left unattended on the sand while everyone's at the restaurant. Even if there's a normally safe dinghy dock, the dink risks getting smashed, punctured, or jammed underneath it—an occasional risk in the BVI's Cane Garden Bay.

If it's not already too late, check the mooring bridle for chafe in places where it touches the boat and be sure to have two, independent, bridles attached to the mooring pendant. If anchored, deploy a second hook or, if space allows, let out more chain to help absorb the up-down motion of the swell.

Since you're on a catamaran consider yourself fortunate or smart in your selection. The cat's motion—particularly rolling—will be unpleasant but much, much less so than if you were on a monohull.

———

PREPARATIONS: Double-check that the boat is not going to drag its anchor or cut through its mooring bridle, secure any loose objects—doors, drawers etc.—and (carefully) prepare something to eat. Think sandwiches or other finger food rather than a proper meal. This is not the time to prepare a gourmet meal, as any loose items on the galley counter or on a table are likely to slide off. Be especially careful of sharp objects and glass bottles. Take care when opening overhead lockers in case heavy cans or plates tumble out on top of you.

HAVE AN EARLY NIGHT. Turn-in and try to get some sleep. If the conditions are still rolly-polly in the early morning, check the wind and wave forecast again, choose a safe haven as the next destination and motor out at first light—after making sure that any open port lights and hatches are closed. Pay particular heed to the channel markers (if any) as you exit.

Get well offshore—at least a mile—before turning parallel to the coast. That experience, while uncomfortable, should remain fresh in your mind when choosing overnight stops in the future!

8

THE BOAT BRIEFING

F or even the most experienced boat jockey, the Boat Briefing is the one essential piece of instruction needed before leaving the safety of the charter base. Charter company staff would normally come your boat and lead you through the on-board equipment and operational procedures. These days, it might be reduced to a YouTube video. There is a lot of information to absorb, so have all crew pay attention. Some will be more interested in the galley, others in the dinghy operation, and so forth. Have the appropriate crew pay special attention to anchoring, engine operation, the electrical panel and so on. Again, ask the briefer if they mind you filming or recording the content of their presentation. At the very least, make notes!

BEAR IN MIND that the briefers have a sequence to follow. One piece of information leads to another, so try to hold any questions until the briefer gets to that topic—once items get out of sequence, things can get skipped over or missed entirely. Take notes when you first board the boat if anything seems puzzling—the location of light switches, how to turn on the refrigeration, and ask the question when the time comes. And don't hold back—if you are not confident you understand an item, ask for more information and make notes as you go. And bear in mind the old adage: The only wrong question is one that wasn't asked.

Some of the most frequent questions concern the following:

BRIDGE:

Chart Plotter: The most important piece of equipment in the cockpit is the chart plotter/ Multi Function Display (MFD). Take the time to understand the proper sequence for loading pages, entering data and saving waypoints and routes, etc. Is the depth gauge reporting feet or meters? Is it adjusted to read from the hull or the waterline? How to engage/disengage alarms? Ask the briefer to locate the instruction manual for the equipment. Often it is buried under a seat cushion in the saloon somewhere. If you can't locate it, go online using the boat's Wi-Fi and download a copy from the manufacturer's web site. If you haven't already done so, go online for the app relevant to the navigation unit and software.

Engine operation: Go over everything from the starting procedure, to the fuel system, to emergency stop procedures. Some boats will have a key start but most now have electronic starts that require a sequence of switching. Make sure you understand it, since it's easy to turn off the ignition with the engine still running—possibly damaging the alternator. See where the fuel refill port is located. And know where the fuel tanks are located, and emergency cut-off valves and switches. Almost all modern power cats now have electronic throttles and gear shifters. Even if you've used one of these before, have your boat briefer take you through it—they don't give the familiar tactile resistance to your hand movements and there's often a slight lag in response which takes a little getting used to. Depending on age and the model of boat being chartered, they may also have buttons (e.g. 'Cruise Control', 'Station', 'Synch', 'Throttle Only', 'Single Lever') that you might be unfamiliar with. Don't touch until you know what it is they do. And be sure to ask if you don't!

> **NOTE**: *Depending on age and the model of boat being chartered, a good estimate of fuel consumption per engine is around 15-20 US gals/hr @ 15 kts, depending on engine size and output, and* propeller pitch. Generators may consume 0.5 - 1.0 gal/hr.

AUTOPILOT: An invaluable item so long as you master its operation. Make sure that all 'working' crew learn the procedures, too. It's not unheard of for a helmsman to inadvertently hit the "Engage/Auto" button and find he can no longer steer the boat—and not be sure why.

> **NOTE**: *Check that the Autopilot is disengaged(i.e. reading* Standby*) when you depart the dock, otherwise you might T-bone the boat across the way. When motoring even short distances, the autopilot is often the preferred helmsman, but it must be monitored by crew.*

DEPTH GAUGE: Is it calibrated to read from the sea surface, or from the transducer (about 1-2 feet below the surface) or some other value? Whichever it is, make sure you know how to calculate your true safe depth for operation. And if it's in meters and you'd prefer it in feet (or vice versa) ask your briefer to change it for you— and watch what they do.

DISTRIBUTION BOARD

Generator operation: Master how properly to start and stop it. Understand from the boat briefer how to changeover inputs and outputs from shore power to generator. Locate the reset button in case the generator quits—usually because of being overloaded—and won't produce any current after restarting. There is generally a push-button reset on a bulkhead panel next to the generator. Also become familiar with the instruments on the saloon breaker panel. Locate the through-hull that feeds cooling water through the generator. You'll need to know which is the dedicated seacock/through-hull for the cooling water intake. This intake is of narrow gauge and is liable to be blocked should there be much free-floating Sargassum-type seaweed around (generally in the summer), so learn how best to clear it.

Air Conditioning: Most charter operators don't allow you to operate the air conditioning while underway—as with the generator, there is a danger of blocking the water intake. And you shouldn't need it as you'll be outside most of the time anyway. And in the winter months it's usually unnecessary if you crack open a hatch or portlight (and close them during a rain squall). But—especially in the summer months—many people find that, once they're at a mooring ball or dock, it feels hot and so the aircon is often humming away in the saloon and cabins. Many folks, too, like the white noise of the aircon when they're sleeping, but the skipper needs to be able to discern unusual noises in the night.

We recommend favoring caution over the comforting hum of machinery particularly when anchored in crowded conditions. Make sure you receive clear instructions on how to operate it during the boat briefing, as it requires either shore power to be connected or the generator on and the power transfer switches turned accordingly.

Battery Charging: Powercats generate lots of amps with their main propulsion engines but you're not going to be motoring all day. Far from it. Meanwhile, fridges and freezers will be drawing 24 hours a day and every time you run the freshwater pump, use the heads, blast the stereo, turn on a light, activate the dinghy davits, drop or (especially) raise the anchor, you're using them up.

So make sure you get proper instruction in battery-charging proce-dures. Before leaving the dock, disconnect the shore power cables and after allowing five minutes for the system to settle, observe the change (if any) from a charging voltage to a resting, or true state. If there is a substantial difference, you may have problems with your batteries. One issue with all charter yachts is that the changing roster of operators week after week means there's no standard manner of charging.

NOTE: *A fully charged 12-volt battery system should be taken to a level of 14.2-14.4 volts initially, if there is no drain on the system. Once the charger is disconnected, the voltage should fall to around 12.8 volts. Don't let it get any lower than 12 volts—even that is too low a charge, about 25% of capacity.*

VHF Radio: Learn the basics of the unit and, if close to US territories, how to get a weather forecast by accessing the WX button—if there is one. A surprising number of VHF units are set incorrectly, so make sure yours actually works properly by performing a radio check with the dockmaster prior to leaving the charter base, or by using your hand-held unit. Know how to make a Mayday call. And make sure as many crew as possible get this briefing since, in a real emergency, some crew could be incapacitated or busy on other tasks.

Bilge pumps: Make a basic map of their locations. Particularly ask to hear them in action. Get all your crew to become familiar with the sound of an active bilge pump. It might indicate a leaking water tank, or it might simply be a stuck float switch—one that needs to be poked with a broom handle or boat hook to reset—so know how many float switches there are and their locations.

Boat papers: If you are planning on going to another jurisdiction—crossing from the BVI to the USVI or Puerto Rico, or from St. Martin to Anguilla or St. Barths, for example—make sure you have the requisite papers. The charter company needs to know beforehand if you're planning such a trip, since it may affect the choice of vessel they supply to you—some individual boats may not fit the regulatory requirements of the island you wish to go to. Request customs forms, too.

You'll need the boat's registration information and, when returning to the original port of departure, you'll need a copy of the cruising permit. These are usually located in the chart table. Make sure there's a chart in there as well! And remember that when clearing in to a new port you'll need your clearance from the previous one. Read the fine print closely, since some forms require many signatures, as well as addresses and other details for all passengers.

Entertainment tech: Power Cats come with a variety of entertainment options from big-screen TV to multi-stage Fusion brand audio players with inputs for direct connectors, Bluetooth, and other technologies. In some cases you'll be able to direct cast from your tablet or phone direct to a big screen or sound system, so ask for a full explanation. If you have a teenager onboard, they might be the best option for gaining rapid insight into the complexities of the system.

First Aid kit: The kit supplied with the boat does not always have the best selection of treatment options. Someone is going to need it at some point since an insect bite, a stubbed toe, sunburn, even a jelly fish sting (or a hangover) are not outside the realms of possibility. Make sure it is fully stocked and have available the additions you brought with you—high quality Band-Aid type plasters, antihistamines, good pain relievers, etc. Keep the kit in an easily accessible place and make sure everyone knows where it is.

Freshwater pump: While most Power Cats come equipped with watermakers, the smaller models may have multiple water tanks that require filling at a marina or fuel dock, so you'll have to switch the manifold valve from one tank to the next. Have your crew become familiar with the sound of the running water pump—it could mean either a leak, a tap left running, or it might indicate that the water tank is empty and the valve needs switching. It is often hard to hear the pump when the generator is running. The water pump can often run "dry" but only for a short period—repeated dry runs day after day may burn out the motor.

Be mindful of water consumption, otherwise you'll be lining up to fill your tanks every other day. In some islands, a trip to replenish water can take several hours.

> **NOTE**: *The Universal Water Rule is: Fresh water lasts in inverse proportion to the amount of hair on the boat.*

If the boat has a watermaker, you'll run it for at least a couple of hours every day. Get a thorough instruction in the intricacies of this equipment. Avoid having all the water-tank valves open at the same time, since the higher tanks can bleed down into the still-full lower tanks, putting immense pressure on the seams—sometimes leading to a breach in the side of that tank and the loss of your potable water.

> **NOTE**: *Even if you have a watermaker, you may not be able to use it in shallow anchorages. The water may contain sand and weed, stirred up by boat traffic or wave action, that can make the watermaker inoperable.*

Inventory: There should be an inventory list or manifest aboard the boat. Go through this thoroughly with the briefer. For two reasons: 1) because you'll be charged for items not on the boat when you return and, 2) most important, it's the best way of learning where everything is.

Refrigeration: All but the smallest Power Cats have separate fridges and freezers. If they're not already clearly labeled, label or otherwise make sure you and your crew know which sliding drawer is the fridge and which the freezer!

For units that combine the fridge and freezer compartments, check the location of the thermostat and that it is properly set. Some boat refrigerators get very cold and can freeze lettuces and other fragile vegetables—not to mention eggs and milk —so learn where the cold plate is. Make it a routine to move items around and/or place a barrier of a small sheet of cardboard (from, say, a wine box) or bubble wrap to prevent items from touching the plate.

Anchor ball: You may plan to never anchor—but you might have to. So locate it and learn how to assemble and raise it. Ask your briefer where it should be attached for greatest visibility. Displaying an anchor ball, as with all signal displays, is not just good maritime practice, it can be a deciding factor in any insurance claim or dispute.

Stove operation/Barbecue grill: On a modern Power Cat, your galley stove/oven, as well as the BBQ grill, may be either electric or propane gas. If the latter, few things are more frustrating than a stove that won't light or won't stay lit. Many stoves and ovens are self-lighting but we recommend you buy a long-barreled stove lighter—one that can reach all the way to the back of the oven. These units vary from boat to boat. Make sure you get a thorough training in how to light it and how to control temperature. By "thorough" we mean have the briefer actually light it—not just point at the controls and give a verbal run-through. This is temperamental equipment—but crucial to the wellbeing of skipper and crew!

Toilets and holding tanks: The marine toilet is possibly the most important piece of equipment on the vessel. Pay close attention to the briefing, since a malfunction can have serious consequences. Most catamarans have the heads en suite and thus have no central units available for general use, so if one toilet goes down, the crew will be obliged to share toilets/showers until the charter company tech support team comes out to fix it. Locate the holding-tank outlet valves. You will be using them pretty much every day, so either make sure the occupants of the relevant cabins learn how to work them, or delegate the task to a single crew or on a rotating roster. Before leaving the dock, check all toilets to see that they are flushing correctly and are free of blockages.

EXTERIOR:

Cockpit lockers: Go through them thoroughly, since this is where you'll find emergency equipment, flares, PFDs, etc. Also swim fins, masks, dive flag, and other useful gear. You may be able to organize lockers so as to stow cases of beverages and other bulky items.

Dinghy security: Learn how to hoist the dinghy in its davits and how to secure it properly to prevent it from swinging side-to-side when hoist. Ask the briefer to supply a length of light line for this if not already provided and to locate and demonstrate the security cable and lock for the dinghy. Lock the dinghy to the mothership every night.

Emergency tiller: If your yacht has one, learn where it is stowed and how it fits to the rudder stock. Ask the briefer to demonstrate how to turn the tiller when the boat is underway (when water is flowing over the rudder, you won't be able to do so without some mechanical assistance).

Windlass and anchor: Learn how to release the clutch to let it free-wheel for quicker anchor dropping. And make sure the release handle for the clutch is always close to hand in case of emergency. If you've brought some colored cable ties with you, attach them at regular lengths, beginning at 20 feet and every 20 feet after. Find the anchor snubber line and ask how to attach the hook to the anchor chain. Also, have the briefer show you how to deploy and retrieve the built-in anchor bridles

9

HEAD MASTERY

THE GAME OF THRONES

Traditionally it's The Heads, or The Head, but let's be bold and call it the toilet. It's the most important piece of equipment on the boat and is as sensitive as an opera star. Treat it like it's #1 and it won't behave like it's #2, OK?

> **NOTE**: *Nothing…NOTHING…goes down the toilet unless it's been through your digestive tract first.*

Well, maybe paper. Small pieces of paper. No wads, no fistfuls. Little pieces, a couple of sheets at a time. And flush between the sheets. No toenail clippings, razors, dental floss, hairclips, rings, tampons, watches, false teeth—you name it, they've all been in there. So please keep all foreign objects out of the bowl. No baby wipes, 'flushable' or not. No hair from the hairbrush. No bits of fluff off your shirt. Nothing but little bits of TP.

The reason is that, on most modern yachts, everything that goes into the toilet has to pass through a very small and weak blender/grinder called a macerator. If things get stuck in the macerator it can't do any macerating. You do not want to listen to your toilet attempting to digest a toothbrush. It's no fun. That means someone has to get down on hands and knees and disassemble the whole shebang and clean it out and re-seal it, which often means unscrewing the toilet base from the floor of the bathroom and generally turning the Throne Room into the Poop Deck. Bad!

MOST OF THE newer units flush with fresh water but most still use salt water. Except for the need to keep your water tanks topped-up, there is no tangible difference as far as you are concerned, but in the long term the fresh water device is a better proposition—less corrosion, less odor.

Almost all the units you will encounter will be electrically filled and flushed via a rocker switch, which pumps water into the bowl and drains the bowl contents through a macerator and into a holding tank. The most common model of toilet also has a separate rinse rocker switch, which does what you imagine it does.

THE PROPER WAY TO use the toilet is, after raising the lid:

- First, pump water into the bowl. Then sit down on the open seat. And Gentlemen, this includes you. Yes, sit, every time.
- Then do your business, whatever form it might take.
- If necessary, wipe the sensitive parts of your body.
- Rather than flush the soiled sheets, place them in the bin. Baby wipes or paper towels go there as well—usually inside a sealable paper or plastic bag. Save plastic shopping bags for this purpose or bring/buy a box of small plastic bin liners. This way you reduce the risk of clogging the macerator.
- Flush away the evidence.
- If the evidence refuses to completely disappear, flush again. And again. Leave it as you'd like to find it.
- When all evidence has disappeared, press the rinse button and then pump out as much water as possible from the bowl so it doesn't slosh around and spill over the lip of the bowl underway.

NOTE: *Flush the bowl empty so there's little to no water in it. Close the seat at all times when not in use—things can fall into the toilet and really jam up the works. That includes baby wipes.*

THE GAME OF THRONES:

Your boat will come equipped with holding tanks that receive and store the black water from the toilets. When you're in bays and harbors—anywhere people are swimming around the boat—keep those tanks closed by way of shutting the valves that you were shown during your boat briefing. It is important that you empty the tanks on a daily or every-other-day basis. Do it when you are en route from one anchorage to the next and as far offshore as you're going to get. Include the evacuation of the holding tanks as part of your daily Passage Plan. And make sure you comply with local regulations regarding discharges—not in National Park areas, for example. And don't empty the tanks while operating the generator while anchored or on a mooring--you might suck the contents into the genny. Bad!

NOTE: *While the valves need to be closed when you next enter an anchorage or marina, it is most important that you return to the base at the end of your charter with the valves draining the holding tanks in the* **open** *position. If you return with full tanks, you will likely be assessed a fee.*

10

ISLAND HOPPING
CLEARING IN/OUT

The islands of the Caribbean are variously self-governing entities, such as Dominica, or overseas dependencies of large nations, such as the Virgin Islands (British or US). Some territories share the same island, such as St. Martin/Sint Maarten. The separate Saba and Statia are affiliated with the Kingdom of the Netherlands and thus the EU. Whenever you leave one jurisdiction and enter another you will be required to file paperwork with either one or both places. Some may require visas but all will require ship's papers, crew passports, their forms filled-in correctly and money—in their local currency.

None of the officers you meet and to whom you'll offer your documents is in any great hurry to rush the process. But don't be tempted to debate any of the requirements or betray too much impatience—you'll only delay the proceedings.

You may feel as if your presence deserves some kind of reward, since you are bringing your hard-earned money to spend in this little piece of Paradise. But to the officials, you are simply a person to whom they may or may not grant the privilege of entry. And it is a privilege, not a right. It's their Paradise, after all.

So be polite and patient and ask a few questions about the best places to see. And don't be in too much of a hurry. It is often to your advantage to begin every conversation with *Good morning*, or *Good afternoon*, in the local language as the first words of your first sentence—there is a formality to the discourse that can be quite endearing.

And, if you find the whole rigmarole just a little ridiculous, don't let on or you might find yourself at the back of the queue wondering what happened. Wait for the reply. Then you could ask something like, is there a restaurant featuring the island's specialties to advantage? Churches are often a fertile topic for conversation—ask if there's one of significance you might visit.

If you are thinking of taking your yacht to a different jurisdiction, the charter company needs to know from the outset. Some companies have restrictions on where you can take their vessels and they may need to supply you with extra paperwork such as the boat's original documentation, import permits, proof of insurance, or they may have to add some extra equipment.

They'll know what's required and whether or not you need to clear out of the country before you leave. They may also need to supply you with a boat that can pass the requirements for entry to that jurisdiction.

Most charter companies will have the yellow Q flag on board but the courtesy flag for the country that you're visiting may not be included in the yacht's standard inventory.

Check before you leave because not flying the correct courtesy flag (or flying it upside down) is, well, discourteous.

———

BEFORE YOU LEAVE the charter base, where you'll have access to a photocopier, make multiple copies of your crew manifest—names, addresses, passport number, and so forth—as some territories require as many as 3 or 4 copies and you may be visiting more than one foreign territory. A trip starting in St. Martin, for example, may also include Anguilla, Saba, and St. Barths—sometimes two in the same day.

WHEN YOU GET to where you're going, make sure that your former courtesy flag is down and exchanged for the yellow Q flag. While unlikely, if your passage took you into international waters, the former should have come down as you left territorial waters.

If you're just planning on staying a day or two then you can ask to clear in and out at the same time, so as to avoid having to come back and do more paperwork before you leave. Most islands allow you to stay 24-48 hours this way, though it varies.

Are the crew permitted to go ashore while the captain is clearing in the vessel? Some island territories are very strict, some are lax and most are reasonable. Check the boat's cruising guide (and websites such as Noonsite.com) for a list of the ports of entry and the exact location and opening hours of the government buildings you must visit.

ALSO, the time of year is important. If you arrive in, say, St. Barths, around New Year you will find it filled to the brim with superyachts and attendant crew, celebrities, and craziness. This is not the best time to present the Customs and Immigration authorities with complications. They are overwhelmed with sensitive issues already. Have all your documents ready, passports open, and a smile affixed. And money in the correct currency! Be prepared to wait. But show up six months later and you'll find the harbor empty, the officials relaxed, and you might even get a space right on the dock.

When going ashore, bring a waterproof bag for carrying documents and passports (it might be a wet dinghy ride to clear in). And don't forget a pen! You might need local currency (Euros, EC dollars, US dollars) to pay entry fees. Not everyone takes credit cards. Prepare for all eventualities.

And after you've cleared in with both Immigration and Customs, and before you wander out to explore the town or have a leisurely lunch, you should send someone back to your boat to take down the 'Q' flag and replace it with the courtesy flag of the country you've now legally entered. Though, if your stay in town is to be brief, it can wait until your return.

11

SHIP'S CHAT
INSTANT MESSAGING

C lear communications aboard ship are crucially important. Wind and engine noise can make it hard to communicate across the length of the vessel. One advantage of the modern Power Cat is the excellent view offered by the high flybridge where the operator is generally located. From that position they can see virtually 360 degrees, though they might have to walk across the deck to see everything. But when approaching a mooring or preparing to release the anchor, the operator can be at a disadvantage, since the closer the vessel gets to the mooring or drop point, the less visible things are.

ONE WAY TO solve the problem is to use a signal system that is simple, clear, and easily understood. Signals are best when uncomplicated, so practice them in the cockpit area before implementing them properly.

The signal should be maintained for as long as the procedure is needed. With an occasional exception—for instance, keep the fist raised and clenched to signal for neutral, but then extend the arm out to indicate the direction to turn the boat.

HERES HOW

MOTOR FORWARD/REVERSE, OR DRIFT IN NEUTRAL?

Neutral: Clenched fist raised at ear height.

Forward: Open vertical palm/tomahawk chop in direction of desired movement at ear height. Increase rate of hand movement to reflect desired speed.

Reverse: A reverse wave of the hand with flat palm facing backwards OR a gentle pat on the buttocks—it may sound silly but it works.

WHICH WAY TO STEER?

- Extend arm and hand in direction boat needs to go.
- Direction to steer in neutral is the steady hand pointing the appropriate way.

DISTANCE OFF DOCKS, NEARBY BOATS AND MOORING BALLS?

The best way for the driver to judge distance off a dock or other obstruction is to have crew stand somewhere within—but not blocking—the field of view from the helm station, with arms fully outstretched. The forward edge of the appropriate hull is usually the best. If the boat is reversing, a crew member standing in the forward position can relay the instructions from the crew member at the stern.

Have them wait until the dock comes to the same distance as their fully outstretched arms (let's say that span is 5' 6" /168 cm) before beginning the procedure. Any distance more than that is not an issue.

As your vessel approaches the dock, the assisting crewmate brings their hands together to indicate the distance-off. This visual representation is clear and precise and can be used when squeezing through a narrow gap in a marina or mooring field—as well as when approaching a mooring ball.

Start the signal at one or two boat lengths off the target— more if there is a lot of traffic or heavy wind affecting progress—when approaching a mooring or anchor drop.

When docking, the first signals may be describing direction and speed but may revert to Distance Off when close to the target. And when docking, the signals person may have to communicate direction, speed and distance-off at the same time!

This person effectively has control of the boat—so sightlines must be clear. When docking, make sure the line handlers don't get in the way. At the same time, the driver is responsible for overall safety and seamanlike decision-making. Right-of-way rules need to be observed at all times.

OTHER USES:

In all cases these signals are generally well understood:

1. Palm of hand raised in the universal traffic cop gesture means: STOP.
2. Thumb raised in universal OK shape signifying Okay or Good.

NOTE: *Spend a few moments with the crew each day making sure they understand the signals and when they should be used.*

12

LOCAL KNOWLEDGE

BOAT BOYS ETC.

Throughout the Caribbean, enterprising entrepreneurs—known everywhere as Boat Boys, though some are female—offer valuable services. Approaching your boat in mooring fields and anchorages (but not marinas) they will offer to sell you ice, take away garbage, and may display a range of provisions.

Sometimes they dawdle on their way and at others they may race against a competitor or two—it depends on the time of day and the season.

Before coming alongside they will usually ask if you want what they have and if you say, 'No thanks,' they'll just move on to the next boat. They will usually not harass you if you don't want what they're selling. There are times, though, when their technique is more insistent.

Whether offering assistance in guiding you to a mooring or displaying a cooler filled with fish, the Boat Boys are eager to close the deal. How you respond is a matter of choice. Sometimes it's simpler to regard the conversation as a form of entertainment. The game is all about removing a few (much needed) dollars from your pocket. Whether it be for a mooring or for a fresh mango or for a watchful eye on your dinghy when you go ashore, some sort of transaction can surely be arranged.

Now, it must be said that—like business folk everywhere—the Boat Boys rely on goodwill and the maintenance of their reputation. It's not in their interest to harass, intimidate, or rob their customer base. Word gets around.

But some sailors would prefer to not have to deal with them. Some sailors just don't like to be bothered. But if you treat the Boat Boys as a resource—the same way they look at you—and ask where to get a taxi or where to find fresh batteries, you might be pleasantly surprised by the response. As citizens of the islands, the Boat Boys do feel proprietary about the place—you, after all, are coming to their home. And they do know everything and everyone.

Boat Boys in Tobago Cays

And everywhere you'll find a number of local kids who might come to your boat offering ice and a garbage pickup. It's surprising how pleased you are to see someone who is offering what you need, when you need it—and how much you look forward to their arrival, even at 7am, before school starts!

As everywhere, folks are hustling to make a living. They see boat after boat, each worth a half-million dollars or more, come into their local anchorage and the hope arises that maybe they can be of service. A few bucks for a bag of ice makes a big difference to these purveyors, so we try to spread some joy where we can.

As HONORABLE AS the majority of Boat Boys are, you might encounter a few rogues. The usual time to meet such a one is when about to drop anchor. Suddenly, a fast speedboat will buzz up on you and a cheery voice will call out, "You can't anchor there, Cap. No. Bottom no good. Come with me."

And he might lead you to a rather dubious looking rope tied to a bleach bottle and say, "Here you go, Cap. Nice secure mooring for you. Only $30."

Now on a night without a breath of wind and minimal current, you might be lucky and get away with it. But if the Cruising Guide suggests there's decent holding in the bay, stay with your first plan and politely—or forcefully, if necessary—go with your original decision

13

TALK RADIO

As the world of electronics grows continually more sophisticated, the gear we see on new boats has grown ever more complex and capable. That trusty standby of marine communication, the VHF radio, now sports many new refinements—though not all of these will be activated on the unit aboard your charter bareboat. But the VHF will be a constant part of your daily routine, so make sure that the boat briefer instructs you in detail how it works. They come from various manufacturers and each has its power, volume, and squelch controls in different places—so familiarity with one brand may not be helpful when faced with a new one. And be sure to do a radio check before you leave the base.

Have a couple of crew sit in on the VHF briefing—they can pass on the knowledge to the others. It is an essential piece of safety equipment and may be a literal life saver. In addition, it will be in use several times each day for making dock or dinner reservations, hailing dive boats, checking weather forecasts, etc.

WHILE WE GENERALLY ADVISE AGAINST relying on your mobile phone for making emergency calls, some Caribbean jurisdictions—the

British Virgin Islands, for one—have emergency services that do not monitor VHF frequencies at all. So if an emergency should arise, use the VHF for an initial call and to monitor responses (with VHF, you may get assistance from a nearby boat, for instance), but also use your phone to call the emergency numbers as provided by the charter

Expect to see emergency information posted to the bulkhead at the Nav station.

In the BVI, channel 16 calls are monitored by US Coast Guard personnel from the US Virgin Islands or Puerto Rico, and requests for assistance may be routed to local BVI responders. But a phone call to the all-volunteer BVI Search and Rescue (VISAR) will probably have a quicker response. (On all bareboats, there is generally a notice stuck to the bulkhead by the navigation station with emergency information for the local sailing area. It will be covered in your briefings as well.)

But it's not only the dire emergency that makes the VHF so useful. We've seen inflatable toys fly off the stern of a boat motoring at speed. A quick call on the VHF to 'Power Cat motoring NE off Fat Man Cay' was enough to get them to turn back and grab the wayward flamingo. So, think of the VHF as not only the best way for you to contact the world, but for the world to contact you.

IN GENERAL THOUGH, the VHF is your go-to communications tool. Its defining feature is that it broadcasts to anyone with a working receiver, whereas phones are one-to-one. This broadcasting capability means that aid may be just as likely to come from a nearby vessel or shore-based assistance, as from an official search-and-rescue or emergency responder. Also, rescue services often are able to create a single line of position from just a few seconds of listening to your MAYDAY or other emergency call.

NOTE: *Learn how to change from High to Low power—not to save electricity but to take up less VHF bandwidth. If the marina is one mile away you don't need to broadcast your request (and hog Channel 16) up to 20 miles away. And learn how to adjust the Squelch control, then leave the setting alone during your charter.*

It makes sense to have electronics that are comfortable to use and whose operation is second nature. So, if you own a handheld unit that you are familiar with, bring it along. It can go ashore with the crew and communicate with the mothership, too. Arranging a pickup, for instance. Just don't forget the charger!

Channel 16 is the universal channel for emergency broadcasts and establishing contact with other vessels or shore-based facilities. It is not a channel for conducting non-essential conversations. Make contact on 16 and switch to 68, 69, 71, or 72. And remember to refer to channel numbers in the form of One-Six, Six-Eight, etc.

Once on Channel 16, you'll hear voice traffic ranging from boats calling marinas, restaurants, and other boats to commercial traffic such as cruise ships or ferries. So Channel 16 is a common, shared resource. Be as brief as possible in establishing contact with the other party before switching to a different channel for the (still brief) conversation. There is a protocol to VHF use that dictates that the party being hailed gets to nominate a channel for both parties to switch to.

LET's say you are on the vessel Rosebud and are calling the restaurant Rotgut's Rodehouse Your exchange would be something like this:

'Rotgut, Rotgut, Rotgut, this is Rosebud, Rosebud, Rosebud. Over.' The response would be something like:

'Rosebud, this is Rotgut. ACKNOWLEDGE and Switch to Channel 68. Over.'

Your response would be, 'Rotgut, this is Rosebud. Switching Six-Eight. Over.'

And you would change the channel selector to Channel 68 and commence calling again.

'Rotgut, this is Rosebud. Over.'

You would expect to hear, 'Rosebud, this is Rotgut. How can I help you? Over.' And you would make reservations for lunch or make inquiries etc.

When you have concluded your conversation, finish by saying 'Rotgut, thank you. This is Rosebud switching back to Channel 16. Rosebud, out.'

THE OBJECT IS to speak clearly, not quickly. Use the term 'Over' at the end of each segment of the conversation, until you've reached the end. Then say, 'Out' to signal that you are concluding the conversation.

Note the triple use of the restaurant's name and the boat's name, initially at least. Is it strictly necessary? In general use, you might only say the name twice, but if you were on the high seas and hoping to attract attention you should indeed follow full protocol and use the triple-term call.

OCCASIONS FOR HAILING ON VHF:

- When approaching a marina and requesting a slip or to pick up fuel and water.

- Making a restaurant reservation. A word of caution: In some areas where there is known to be serious crime we would suggest not using your real boat name when calling in, since that could alert possible thieves to your movements. Just use a simple name for the reservation. A friend always calls his boat Mango II, whatever its real name might be. When making an emergency call, or requesting assistance, however, always use the proper name!
- Calling another boat whose name you know, or hailing a party ashore that is operating a handheld VHF unit.
- Responding to a call from someone whose name you don't know or didn't hear clearly. Use the formula 'Vessel calling Rosebud, please go ahead.'
- When you are traveling in a convoy with friends, or have another boat you wish to stay in contact with, choose a non-assigned channel—09, 68, 69, 71, for example—as a place to conduct conversations. Ask which is the best to use at the base before you leave. You can continuously monitor this channel along with Ch. 16 and any others you wish.

Some areas give the weather forecast in French or Spanish only. The forecast may refer to the Beaufort Scale, such as in the French West Indies where you might hear: 'Nor-est, Cinque, Deux Metres,' (Wind from the North-east, Force 5 or 17-21 knots, Swell—2 meters or 6.4 feet) for example. When communicating with authorities, you will be expected to use the Standard Phonetic Alphabet. Find the Alphabet and much other useful information in our Safety Packet. Since boats get named the strangest things, it may be crucial to know how to spell out your boat name using the phonetic alphabet whether you're booking a table at a restaurant or request immediate helicopter evacuation.

DISTRESS PROCEDURE:

There are levels of urgency associated with emergencies. Some situations require immediate response since a life may be at risk from heart attack, loss of blood, or other trauma. But others, while serious, may not require absolutely immediate response.

Take the example of a vessel under power and getting tangled in some loose fishing nets or hitting floating debris—and knocking out the rudder or jamming the propeller. The vessel may not be able to steer, or may have very restricted capability. Help is required but the boat is afloat and all aboard are safe. A third example is where you wish to convey important information related to safety, such as the presence of a number of floating logs or a sudden squall or waterspout of unexpected severity. In the first instance, the Channel 16 call would be a Distress call, or Mayday. In the second, an Urgent call, or Pan-Pan. The third is a Safety call, or Securité (pronounced Securitay).

MAYDAY:

Don't use this unless there truly is a life-threatening emergency—it could be an allergic reaction/ anaphylactic shock from a jellyfish sting, cardiac arrest, or having to abandon a sinking vessel.

A yacht aground on soft sand in calm conditions wouldn't warrant a Mayday. Though it would if the skipper subsequently suffered a heart attack! When requesting a Mayday response, you are asking for aircraft, helicopters, rescue divers—it's an emergency after all.

The person receiving the call will want to know a lot of information. So when going offshore you should have the information available for immediate access by your crew. It's best presented as a printed card and kept taped to the underside of the chart table top, or someplace close by the VHF station.

WE HOPE you never have to make such a call but if you do, follow this procedure:

First, make sure that your VHF is actually turned on and tuned to Channel 16. Select 25 Watts/HI Power, as you want to broadcast far and wide.

Wait for a gap in conversation if other people are talking and at the first opportunity press the transmit/talk button on the side of the handset. Everyone else making routine calls will stop talking after you say the following words. If people keep talking, don't wait for them to pause but begin with **BREAK, BREAK, BREAK.**

THEN SAY SLOWLY AND CLEARLY:

MAYDAY, MAYDAY, MAYDAY, then (without waiting for a response):

WHO you are (vessel's name)

WHERE you are (Your position in Latitude /Longitude from the chart or GPS, or a bearing and distance from a widely known geographical point.)

WHAT is wrong (nature of distress or difficulty).

KIND of assistance desired.

NUMBER of persons aboard and condition of any injured.

SEAWORTHINESS status of your vessel

DESCRIPTION of your vessel—length, type, cabin, mast, power (sail or motor), color of hull, charter company that you're with, superstructure and trim (listing, foundering etc).

RADIO channel you are monitoring. It's important to make a communications schedule.

SURVIVAL EQUIPMENT available (i.e.. rafts, etc.)

> **NOTE:** *It is important that you give the full range of information since conditions could change and you lose power to your radio. A mariner listening*

may have a chance to write down the information or it could be received by a Coast Guard unit that records all Channel 16 traffic.

Release the transmit/talk button and wait for acknowledgment. Keep listening on Channel 16 for instructions. Appoint a crew member to monitor the VHF for response.

If no response is forthcoming, then repeat the distress call.

Of course, if you should hear a MAYDAY call, write down salient details that you could pass on to the appropriate parties. Respond to the MAYDAY call to:

Confirm to the caller that someone has heard them, and

Gather information that you might be able to pass on by calling the Coast Guard on Ch. 16.

NOTE: *The original caller's signal might be able to reach you but not strong enough to be picked up 50 miles away by Coast Guard antennas.*

RADIO CHECK

The radio check is an important part of familiarization with your equipment. It is not a test you need to make every day. Do it once on the dock with the base operator. The first test is simply to ascertain that the unit is functional. On the dock you'll probably hear back from the dockmaster who might be a few boat lengths away.

The usual procedure is this:

- Set your unit to Low (power), adjust the Squelch setting and go to Channel 16 where you say:
- 'Any station, any station. This is Mango, Mango, looking for a radio check. Over.'
- Ideally you will get a response like this:

- 'Vessel calling for a radio check, this is Tuna, Tuna Receiving you loud and clear from Turtle Cay.'
- 'Loud and Clear' may also be expressed as paired numbers from 1 to 5 as in, '3X5' (moderate volume/maximum clarity) though '4X5' or '5X5' are the general responses. 'Turtle Cay' is wherever the responding vessel is located. Now you have a good idea of the state of the call and the distance it can be heard. You may get several responses. All the better.

NOTE: *We say Ch.16 for the radio check. In areas other than the Caribbean we might suggest 68 or 72 but in the islands there isn't a lot of traffic on those channels so you might not get any responses. Ch.16 is a good option in this instance. Of course, if there is traffic on Ch. 16, use 68 or 72 etc.*

14

CAT POWER

In the world of recreational boating, the differences between sailors--that is mariners who like to ride around on boats with a mast and sail--and those who prefer a boat which provides its own propulsion, are wide and often thought insurmountable. However with the changing boating demographic and the reduction in pleasure craft ownership, the number of people choosing to charter has increased dramatically. As we mentioned earlier, the offerings in the charter market have also increased in number and type. Boats are bigger, more comfortable, and easier to operate.

A lot of sailors now move easily from monohulls to catamarans for the increased comfort and space. Many of these have moved further —from sailing catamarans to power catamarans—and many more dedicated powerboaters have started to charter in areas that were traditionally the home of wind-powered sailors. This increase in interest in the power end of the catamaran market has meant that the number of boaters coming from different starting points have ended up in the same place: At the helm of a Power Cat. It is possibly the fastest growing segment of the market today.

Operating a catamaran under power is a very precise operation. The widely spaced engines coupled with the shallow draft mean you have the torque to turn the vessel 360 degrees in its own length. The very same shallow draft coupled with a high superstructure can mean the vessel is sometimes blown around in strong winds, however. But powerful engines can help.

One contrast between the sailing catamaran and the Power Cat is in the engine room. Let's take two boats from the same designer and manufacturer—in this case, a 43-foot LOA Power Cat and 44-foot LOA sailing cat: The PC is listed with 2X 260 HP engines, the sailing cat with 2X 29 HP engines. Displacement of the PC is given as 30,700 bs/13,389 kg. The sailing cat's displacement is 32,930 lbs/14,900 kg.

The difference lies in performance: the sailing cat might motor at 8 or 9 knots while the power cat will cruise at twice that and max out somewhere in the low 20 knots, though some companies do restrict the RPMs to keep speeds down.

But for many cruisers, this constitutes a safety margin. Far better to outrun the weather at 20 knots than at 8. The extra speed will cost you, however. At 15 kts, the 43-foot Power Cat might burn around 26 liters/hr (7 US gals) per engine, at 3000 rpm.

IN GENERAL, the longer the catamaran's waterline, the smoother the ride will be. Short waterlines can lead to pitching, or "hobby-horsing," in swell or chop. Charter groups often load their cats with plenty of toys, which can cause complications if items such as SUPs (Stand-Up Paddleboards) are not properly attached to railings or deck fittings. A sudden squall can tear those items loose and send them flying—which is true of towels, swimsuits, coffee cups and all kinds of small items. Keep them tied off or tidied away. And, when underway upwind at perhaps 16 knots, against a typical True Wind of 15 kts, the resulting 30+ knot airflow on deck will blow more than the froth off your Painkiller. It could be more or less, depending on the prevailing wind, so the risk is always present. It is a good idea to appoint someone to supervise the "deck risk" and make sure all loose items are secured.

Now, it is obviously true that every sailing boat is a powerboat—at least until the sails go up. And even then charter company research has shown that many people who charter sailing yachts often simply drive them around under power anyway and seldom operate under sailpower alone. That makes sense because on a 7-Day sailing vacation, the probability of the wind blowing from the optimum direction at the optimum strength is highly variable. So why not motor? And many catamaran sailors are not comfortable when sailing close to the wind, so they motor for a good part of the time, anyway. Consequently, if you are going to motor, why not do so in a vessel that's built to do that?

Then the question now is:

How do you operate a Power Cat?

Are there differences between the Power Cat and a more traditional power boat?

Are there differences between a Power Cat and a regular sailing catamaran (other than the horsepower of the motors)?

Let's take a look.

First, there are two types of Power Cat. One variety is basically the same form as a deep-V monohull power vessel but with the hull split into two, lengthwise. This is properly known as a Twin-V or twin-hulled boat. The physics involves air and water compressed within a narrow open space between the hulls and is seen in smaller (mid 20-30 feet) ocean fishing boats.

The type of Power Cat that you'll be aboard is derived from the sailing catamaran hull shape and presents a beam of about double the width of a comparable length monohull. This is the ideal shape for a charter yacht, providing large amounts of accommodation within a relatively short Length Overall.

One obvious difference between the Power Cat and other motor-driven vessels is that it occupies a niche somewhere between a displacement power yacht—such as a trawler—and a planing vessel —such as a sports fisherman—that climbs up on its own bow wave and, while fast, burns lots of fuel.

The fact is that the PC is a bit of a hybrid—in part it's somewhat of a displacement yacht and at the same time has some characteristics of the planing vessel. It is technically, a *semi-planing, semi-displacement* vessel. The Power Cat sits largely on the water rather than in the water and because of its widely spaced engines is highly maneuverable—and because of its light weight is highly responsive to the throttle. So the driver of the Power Cat has to learn to be very gentle and precise with the electronic throttle because

- there is a slight delay between movement of the controls and response from the engine and the boat might surge ahead if too much power is applied, causing discomfort and possible injury to an unwary crew member or guest. And
- because the throttle controls lack the friction inherent in cable-led controls and so offer no resistance to inputs— making it likely the operator might apply too much grunt inadvertently.

ONE WAY of handling the throttle is to wrap a finger and thumb around the base of the electronic control lever--almost like holding a pen or pencil—and bracing with the extended fingers against the console or throttle housing.

This allows for quite firm control over the movement of the throttle. Very small movements of the throttle will result in sharp increases of power at the propeller. As there are two throttles, two hands need to be working at the same time—unlike, say, a displacement vessel, where a heavy hand on the throttle will be counterbalanced by the large weight of the boat,which will be slow to respond.

And in similar fashion the light weight of the Power Cat and its small wetted surface area will allow it continue to glide after power is reduced. But a short burst on the engines will slow it right down. So you have to be careful with the throttles then, too, to avoid a herky-jerky response.

As with many power boats, most of the time when under way you'll be on autopilot, particularly when on charter in sheltered conditions. But this is not simply a matter of *set and forget*—you have to keep an eye open and be aware of how you've set your autopilot.

Are you following a set course or heading to a waypoint?

In the first instance you may be following a course—let's say 200 degrees (true or magnetic). You may be following your 200 degrees but be effectively offset several degrees sideways across your course by force of wind or current. And bear in mind that 1 knot of current can be equal to 15-30 knots of wind (depending on the angle of the wind, the temperature of the air and other variables).

Or if headed to a waypoint, you may still be going as you intended, but your course is now extending over a reef you weren't expecting or towards an island that is now between you and your destination —it wasn't in the way when you initially plotted your course but you drifted in the current.

We know of a couple who set their autopilot knowing they had four hours to reach their destination. At some point they both fell asleep and they unfortunately ran the boat up onto a beach. But they were professionals, so it probably wouldn't happen to you.

WHERE THE BOAT operation may become complicated is when you are punching into waves or swell, or even operating in gusty winds. That's when you will have to use the throttles to maintain your angle to the swell or to combat the force of the water and/or the wind.

Operating the Power Cat in such conditions can be challenging. The boat's separated hulls, elevated superstructure and lack of draft/depth in the water mean you can get slammed by water forced up between the hulls pushed around in a brisk breeze.

As the wave/wind force increases so also does the onboard discomfort and the effort required to stay on course. The catamaran shape also means the boat will roll from side to side and perform like a rocking horse in even a medium-size swell. This rock and roll behavior means that passage planning is an even more important aspect of your charter. You don't want to upset the family or your guests by bouncing around in wild conditions all afternoon. And, given that the usual driving position on the Power Cat is from the upper deck/flybridge, you don't want to feel as if you are on a roller coaster while trying to control the boat.

IF YOU WANT to continue on, you'll have to slow down. Alternatively, perhaps, head to a destination downwind (though not dead downwind—you need to be at a shallow angle to the swell). And if the swell and wind are from differing directions, be careful.

It might be a good day to stay where you are (if well sheltered) and explore the shore-side amenities. One advantage of the Power Cat is that you can change your mind easily and head off in a different direction from your original one. Or make a few short local trips and return to your sheltered starting point whenever you like.

15

WET WORK
HEAVY WEATHER

W hen we talk about heavy weather in the Caribbean we're talking about one of two things:

- Strong to Gale or even Storm force winds resulting from a major meteorological system. This is a macro-scale event that'll be well forecast. Or,
- A Squall. These are comparatively micro-scale weather events that will not be forecast any more than the routine Caribbean forecast of isolated showers.

WHEN CHARTERING, you're unlikely to get caught in a hurricane—or even a named storm. These are tracked for days and are well forecast. Your charter company will have called you back to base or directed you to a safe haven before one reaches you. And if you were so unfortunate, all charter companies credit you any days lost due to named storms.

Squalls are much more common and much less easy to predict. You are bound to at least see one in the distance if not get caught up by one. They can be isolated to a small area covering just a few square miles and lasting just five, ten, or fifteen minutes, though it might feel like longer!

If you're observant, you can often steer around—or outrun—an approaching isolated squall and miss it completely. Watch for vertical development and note whether the high tops (anvil-shaped) are directly above the base or inclined more to the left or right. If they're inclined right, the squall is going right (so head left to avoid it) and vice versa. If it's getting taller and darker and lined-up straight then it's coming directly at you.

Another type of common squall is the Line Squall. These are less easy to avoid because, well, there's a line of them. But they too are often short-lived, despite their ominous look as they get closer and closer. Apart from the wall-to-wall line, these squalls are distinguished by causing all the local sea birds to fly away as, like you, they can't fly around the line. You can't fly with them so you've got three choices—plow on into it and get it over quickly, control the vessel with throttle and varying engine thrust so as to stay pretty much where you are, or turn away to reduce the apparent wind and position the gusts and waves on your quarter rather than crashing over your bows.

If the squall seems especially severe, it might be best to use the engines to keep the boat pointed as close to the wind as possible, either maintaining your ground position or moving forward at 1 or 2 knots to basically hold your ground until the squall passes. When either one of these squalls gets close to you (about one mile away) you'll first notice a 10-20% increase in windspeed. This will happen before it starts to rain.

One complication in this situation is the wind pressure on the common wrap-around curtains on many Power Cats. These Eisenglass-style curtains roll up and are secured to the edge of the hardtop—but when there is water in the air or even excess wind, they can be rolled down and snapped or zippered into place. They provide excellent shelter but they also present a solid face to the wind and can contribute to the difficulties in controlling the boat in heavy weather.

The alternative is to not deploy them--but then the occupants of the exposed upper deck are subject to lashing rain and wind. And the control panel, seating, and other exposed elements receive a good soaking. The instruments are designed to take driving rain but if you haven't donned them already, this is the moment that you wish you'd packed a Gore-Tex jacket and swim goggles! (We mention Gore-Tex a few times—not because we have an interest in the company but because it is an excellent product used by a number of top-level outdoor outfitters.)

So, the first action when the weather turns hostile is to clear the exposed decks of extraneous personnel. Turn on your navigation lights and post a dedicated lookout—someone who's also got some weather resistant clothing and eye protection—and get your PFDs on. You wouldn't want anyone to slip on the wet surfaces without one!

Then get everyone else down below in the saloon, where they will be comfortable and dry. But make sure there is a way to communicate from one deck to the other. This is where the hand-held VHF unit you brought with you comes in handy—you may need to ask for assistance if things break loose (as they sometimes do) or you need help to perform a task or you want a second opinion when trying to maintain a lookout. Or you just need to take a break for a few minutes. It's best if there's a second crew member on the bridge at all times.

NOTE: *If you are in the line of an oncoming squall, copy your lat/long position from the chart plotter and write it down— you'll need to mark it on your paper chart. This is another good reason to have brought your handheld GPS unit, since the squall may produce lightning and there is a chance your boat electronics could be affected. You'll need to track course and speed (from the compass and by estimate) and plot them on your chart—or use the information to create a dead reckoning position. Where there is minimal visibility, you'll need to know where you are in relation to land.*

Your charter yacht likely won't have radar or a radar reflector and while you may be a mile or two offshore, there could be ferries and other power craft in the vicinity. You might be traveling 2-3 knots even if you're barely powering—so keep your nav lights on and maintain a look out.

16

M.O.B RULES
DON'T GO OVERBOARD

The question of what to call the person in the water has colored much of the discussion of how best to retrieve the accidental swimmer. Whether it's a man, woman, child or crew, the correct terminology is probably Person—but Man Over Board is still the most common expression for this circumstance in the English-speaking nautical world. And MOB is what the label on your chart-plotter's emergency button will say. So we'll stick with those.

In reality, the Power Cat is one of the least likely platforms to lose a crew member overboard. This is largely because there is so little exposure for crew while underway—no sail handling—but it is still a possibility. The solid rails along the side decks of the Power Cat are an asset, too.

But there are ladders and steps to negotiate on the multi-level Cat, and a mis-timed foot—or an attempt to perform a maneuver with hands full—can set in motion a tumble or slip that can put someone in the water. Most likely on a day that is wet, bouncy, and blustery.

In just one minute, assuming a sedate speed of 12 knots or so, your MOB could be 400 yards/meters away. Could you spot your friend or loved on in the midst of the white caps and curling waves from that distance?

While the Power Cat driving position is high and offers 360 degree sightlines, the helm is generally to the forward end of the upper deck/flybridge and either to port or starboard. Those sightlines won't be as clear now. And there might be 20 knots of wind—or more.

WE WILL ASSUME that the prudent skipper would have rehearsed his or her crew in MOB procedures on Day One of the charter. If not, tsk tsk.

- The first essential the crew should learn is to immediately shout as loudly as possible: "MAN OVERBOARD". The person who made the call should immediately point with arm firmly outstretched (so there's no doubt) at the MOB.
- If the pointer is in a position that is hidden from the person driving the boat, another crew member should also point so the driver can see what is going on. Have them stand or sit high in a secure manner somewhere within your own field of vision. This way you only have to look at the spotter and not frantically crane your neck to look for the MOB yourself.
- The spotter must never take their eyes off the MOB or try to help in any other way because the instant they lose sight of the swimmer, it can be very hard to re-establish visual contact. And they must continue to point in the direction of the MOB without distraction. So don't give this person another job to do!
- Throw something floaty. The horseshoe or round lifebelt (PFD) that will be attached to the guardrails close to the after deck is ideal but it's sometimes fiddly to detach, so chuck some cushions as well (provided they are of a conspicuous color!).

- They should be easier to get to and large enough to see. Throw anything else that floats—life jackets, fenders—anything that will create a visual reference. You can always retrieve them later.
- Slow the boat and turn towards the MOB. This person is very vulnerable. Make sure the boat is turned so as to keep upwind of the victim—so any line that is thrown will land easily and not get blown away.
- Be very careful to keep any thrown line well clear of the PC's propellers.
- The Power Cats have a high freeboard so any recovery will need to take place at the transom, putting the MOB very close to the boat's propeller.
- Make sure the transmission driving the propeller closest to the MOB is in neutral.
- Have a crewmember lower the swim ladder on the appropriate side—though be aware that some boats have only one ladder, so you will need to position the boat appropriately.
- When the MOB is close, throw a line so they can be pulled to the ladder. If they are on the "wrong" side of the boat (where there is no ladder), get a line to them and pull them across—or allow them to pull themselves across if they are able.
- Once the victim is alongside and the transmission in neutral help them maneuver to the transom of the boat close to the ladder.
- They may need assistance to get out of the water, so appoint crew to stand by and help. If there's any swell, the boat will be pitching up and down and the swim ladder may quickly become a hazard—and you don't want any more crew in the water!
- There will need to be several crew available to grab an arm or try to get a length of dock line around the victim to help pull them up. Get them out of wet clothes and/or wrap a

towel around them to prevent hypothermia. The combination of a stiff breeze and a wet body can reduce body temperature rapidly, even in the tropics.

Practice makes perfect, so practice it at least once during your charter. It only takes a few minutes and will give you peace of mind. A wind-blown hat going over the side makes the best practice as it happens as unexpectedly as a real MOB.

CAN YOU USE THE DINGHY?

Why not just get in the RIB dinghy?

First, your dinghy is most likely in davits. Launching into a turbulent sea is not an easy task. And, if in davits, it may not have its engine attached, since on some cats the dinghy motor can drag through the rooster tail streaming from between the hulls at high speed. In St Martin and some other Caribbean bases, the charter companies insist that the dinghy engine be lifted and placed on the boat's dedicated pad on the pushpit, or stern rail.

Second, getting into the dinghy in open water can be a challenging business—the dinghy may be bouncing around in chop, for example. The dinghy's engine may not start first time and in your rush to try, you may flood it. Or, someone may enthusiastically release the painter and send you drifting. And can you see the victim now that you're lower to water level?

Can you handle a RIB in waves? Get the victim back in a dinghy? It's not as easy as it seems—especially when the victim is fully clothed.

Then there's the dinghy propeller, which is just inches below the surface. Props and people are not a good combination.

So, No to the dinghy. Yes to practicing the MOB maneuver. It's a fundamental part of a sailor's repertoire, and it will help bond your crew. Hopefully you'll never have to utilize it—most sailors who have spent years on the water may have never had to experience a real MOB. But someday it'll happen—maybe to you. Are your crew ready for that?

17

HOOKING DOWN
ANCHOR WITH CONFIDENCE

A t some point, you're going to want to change rhythm and stop sailing. After first prepping the crew on the upcoming procedures and having dropped sail and tidied up the deck, you may be ready to stop for lunch or overnight in one of the secluded bays and coves that bejewel the Caribbean.

In which case you'll want to anchor. Or it may be that you arrived too late to get a mooring ball—or the only mooring ball left looks a bit dubious. Then you're going to *have* to anchor.

It's not so hard—all you're really doing is dropping onto the seabed a heavy metallic object that won't move, with a line tied to it that is attached to the boat. There are a few variables—where you drop the anchor, how much cable you put out in how much water, and so on. But really, how hard can it be? (*Cue riotous laughter!*).

Well, actually it's pretty simple if you take your time—it may take up to half an hour or more to get the boat properly settled on the hook—and do it carefully.

And let us say right up front—never be afraid to pull up the anchor and reset it if you're not entirely satisfied with your position. It won't take all that long and the peace of mind will be well worth the extra effort. Sometimes it just means dropping the anchor 10 yards/meters further ahead or a bit to the side.

Those small changes can have a large impact on how the boat lies to the wind and how much space you have around you. We have happily reset our anchor several times before we were satisfied—mostly when we expected a big blow to head our way, but sometimes just to avoid coming too close to a neighbor. It's no fun to be eating dinner with your neighbor sitting within earshot—especially when you're listening to some uplifting choral music and they're head-banging like crazy. Or vice versa!

PREPARING TO ANCHOR:

First, check the supplied cruising guide and supplementary charter company notes, which will tell you whether any anchoring restrictions apply. If you see no other boats anchored, ask yourself what might be the reason? You could be the first person to arrive at a less frequently visited bay—or you might be trying to anchor in an untenable or notoriously dangerous spot.

Deck crew indicate approach to anchorage

Your chart—whether paper or chartplotter—may have anchor (as well as no anchoring) symbols but these are provided for vessels of all types—with varying amounts of anchor cable—from small craft to cruise ships.

Your cruising guide will have much more detailed and useful information on the best spot to anchor a recreational craft, such as the one you're on, in the bay of your choice. It'll tell you the water depth and—just as important—the nature of the seabed and what's ashore. If the bay you fancy isn't mentioned in the cruising guide, there may be a good reason why not—so don't assume that you're the first to discover a brilliant new spot.

Then again, just because it's not mentioned doesn't mean it's not a viable possibility. There are many very good anchorages that are only suitable for one or two boats at a time—and sometimes the authors of the guidebooks may have chosen to keep some spots a secret. But don't be too bold about dropping the hook in an unfamiliar and undocumented spot—it might be a very bad decision. If in doubt, make a quick phone call to the charter company base.

Next, assess the all-important wind direction. Although the general wind direction in the Caribbean is from the east (more NE in winter, more SE in summer) the wind direction where you're anchoring may be quite different—maybe even 180 degrees different.

THIS IS because most island anchorages are on the sheltered, leeward side of a headland or other body of land. The eddies this land creates can cause the local winds to vary from the general pattern.

If you're the first or only boat in your bay of choice, you'll have to figure this out yourself, but often someone is there ahead of you.

Aside from being an obstacle to avoid, this vessel is serving as your local direction indicator for how you'll need to align your boat before dropping your hook. If there are several boats, choose the one nearest where you plan to drop.

Generally, catamarans and power yachts lie differently to the wind than deeper-keeled sailing monohulls so, if there's a conflict, align with the boat that's more like the one you're on—i.e.another PC or sailing catamaran And if the direction that the boats lie is unrelated to the local wind, that might indicate some current—which, while generally slight, may be significant twice a month—at times of full and new moon.

NOTE: *Sometimes there are both wind and current in an anchorage or mooring field but the direction that the boats closest to you are pointing is always the direction of that combined wind and current.*

IF you have to anchor close behind another boat, don't be afraid to motor up very close to their stern. Drop the hook a few feet behind —say 10 feet or less—and you'll fall back safely and snug up. In the morning, if you need to weigh anchor before the boat in front is ready to move, they will probably motor ahead by a boat length or so to give you room to maneuver. If they've left the boat and gone to dive or hike on land, you can pull up close, with anchor cable reeled in and, after snubbing the chain, motor astern and drag the anchor free.

Or, use your dinghy to nudge the other boat to one side for a few minutes whilst you pull the hook. These latter techniques may also come in handy after a wind or current shift, or if someone anchors after you and has fallen back to float above your anchor.

Overall, though, the most important factor when anchoring is to give yourself plenty of time. Arriving late to an anchorage and being obliged to find a spot before the sunlight disappears is often an anxiety-inducing situation.

NOTE: *Plan your afternoon arrival before you begin sailing each day. Work backwards, setting waypoints to indicate the passage of time—and give yourself an absolute deadline to make sure you get to the anchorage in good daylight. It may sound excessive, but you'll find the sun sets around 1800 hrs* *in the middle of winter (aka high season). And in the tropics, the sun goes down like flipping a switch. In 20 minutes everything's dark.*

UPON ARRIVAL at your chosen destination, if you don't feel comfortable about your options, then move to another anchorage. Plan to arrive no later than 1500 hours (3:00pm). You need the sun to be still somewhat high in the sky—and remember the sun sets around 1750-1900 (5:50-7:00pm). In some bays, you'll be anchoring in 15-20', enabling you to see the bottom in order to drop your anchor in the light-colored sand rather than the darker sea grass. At other times you'll be in deeper water, up to 30', and not able to see the bottom clearly.

Check your cruising guide to ensure your chosen spot is a safe one for overnight anchoring and proceed in the knowledge that it's been tried and tested by boats with older, less secure anchors than you've got on board your modern bareboat with its new pattern, quick-setting anchor.

SCOPE IT OUT:

The general rule of thumb for anchoring usually advises a 5-to-1 scope for chain and 7-to-1 for line. In the Caribbean you'll have mostly chain anchor cable with possibly a few feet of nylon attached to the chain locker fitting.

So if you want a number, go with 4 times the depth measured from the bow-roller as a minimum.

> **NOTE**: *Another rough formula for the average 45-50' boat is: "Boat length plus double the depth" as applying the often-cited 4-5 times the depth would often not be enough at the shallower depths Caribbean bareboaters are restricted to.*

For example, at 10 ft water depth (found off Anegada, BVI) 45 ft plus 20 comes out at 65' (while simply 5 x 10' depth would have you let out just 50 ft. When in doubt, let more out—(provided you have swing room.) These numbers are minimums, *not maximums.*

Bear in mind that some charter companies calibrate their depth-sounders to show depth under the keel rather than the actual depth from below water level. (Check with your Boat Briefer before departing). The bow roller may be a good 2 meters or more above the water line.

Point the boat head-to-wind or current as indicated by nearby boats, in order to drift the boat to a stop at the right spot. Use a short blast of reverse if you have to.On a catamaran you'll be able to hold the boat steady with your two engines—but drop the hook straight away. Do this using the anchor windlass remote control or by using a winch handle to release the windlass clutch. The windlass will drop the hook slowly (about one foot per second/1 meter every 3 seconds) but using the clutch release will send it down like the lump of metal it is.

In a stiff breeze you're much better off using the clutch release to drop your hook—even though you'll hold the boat fairly straight into the wind, your vast amount of windage will still push the cat around. When dropping the anchor by easing the windlass clutch, be extra careful not to catch vulnerable fingers and other parts in the machinery.

WINDLASS CLUTCH QUICK DROP:

Allow the wind to push the boat's bows back and away while letting out more chain—whilst applying power to either engine to keep the boat straight into the wind. Make sure you don't give too much power to the engines because you might end up holding a stationary position—rather than falling back—and drop your chain in one big pile on the seabed rather than stretching it out. Use short bursts on the throttle rather than a prolonged application of power. Look 90 degrees sideways and make a transit with two in-line objects to check your movement.

Most bareboats have 50 meters (164') of chain spliced to 10 meters (33') of nylon. You don't really want to use the nylon unless you have to, so 30' of water depth is pretty much your limit for safe overnight anchoring, assuming a well-set anchor in good holding ground.

But you shouldn't need to push this limit since catamarans draw so little. Just be careful that you have enough swing room should the wind direction do a 180-degree shift as can occasionally happen during the passing of an isolated squall. And, if you do have plenty of sea room, let more chain out—say 30 feet (10 meters)—for added security. "Better out than in!"

Unlike mooring balls, whose swing radius is defined by your boat length plus your mooring bridle, (and dinghy plus its painter—once you've put it in the water!) when anchored you'll be swinging around what's known as the *lift point*. This is the point at which your chain lifts off the seabed toward your bow.

The stronger the wind and/or current, the closer the lift point will move toward your anchor and the greater your swing radius will be. If you're anchored close to similar boats, with similar length of chain out, then you should all swing together and stay separated.

Problems arise when you're near a boat with a profile different from your own. If you're next to a sailing monohull they will have more boat in the water than out of it while your profile will be reversed and so you will swing more readily to the wind than they. This is a good reason to stay as separated as you can to start with, and also try to anchor near boats like yours. And, of course, your catamaran needs less water depth than the monohull, generally speaking.

Many bareboats have poorly marked anchor cables, making it tricky to judge how much chain you have out. Since you'll almost always have more chain out of the boat than in it, one simple way is to open up the anchor locker and estimate how much chain you have left. If you know that the boat has 160-odd feet (the standard 50 meters most bare boats have) and it looks like you've got 20 feet left, then you have 140' out. Or, you could make your own marks in the chain with brightly colored cable ties (aka zip-ties) if you've had the foresight to bring them with you.

THE POWER SET: This technique both ensures that the anchor is set in good holding ground and helps set it a bit deeper. Too many Power Cat bareboaters, who have heard about this "power set" thing go straight to it—with some, er, power. On a 21st Century Power Cat, with its electronic throttles and turbo diesels driving big propellers this can result in pulling what would otherwise be a perfectly set anchor straight out of its holding. The key is to first let the natural forces of wind and current do their job for a minute or two while sighting two fixed objects (one near, one further away—called a "transit") at right angles to you. Then put the engines into reverse (with the wheel centered) at the lowest possible revs (usually 900/1,000 rpm). Make sure the clutch on your windlass is tightened up, or the locking safety plate is in place. Check for backwards dragging using your transit. Gradually—100 rpm at a time with at least a 10 second pause between each step—increase the rpm until you are still holding tight at around 1,500 rpm. Unless the evening's forecast is dire, don't go any higher as the vessel's powerful engines could pull out the now perfectly set anchor.

Once the Power Set has proved that your anchor is holding, rig your bridle/snubber line (the chain hook attached to lines leading to the forward end of each hull) to take the pressure off the windlass. Rigging this hook around the chain can be tricky, since you often have to slide a hand and forearm through a small slot to access the chain, so be patient. And be aware of the dangers of catching exposed body parts as the boat yaws around the tight chain. But it has to be done, so do it with care. If you skip it, not only will you yaw over closer to neighboring boats but you will have a herky jerky night with periodic "snatch" on the chain each time the boat yaws over to its maximum left and right (at least once a minute).

When the bridle hook is in place, the resulting pivot point will be quite a bit forward of your bows and quite low to the water. That's a bonus good thing!

GPS anchor alarms are useless here as you're mostly so close to rocks and other boats that the sound of them rubbing against your hull will wake you up before your alarm goes off. Not to mention the likelihood of losing your GPS fix momentarily during the night —a constant occurrence—will mean a false alarm in the wee small hours.

If you have one onboard, assemble and raise an anchor ball some-where high, such as the flybridge hardtop support, or the short mast that supports the anchor light. This black plastic folding signal shows—in daylight—that you're anchored, not underway.

At sunset, turn on your anchor light but don't forget to turn it off in the morning. If, as is sometimes the case, the anchor light isn't work-ing, try and make do with the steaming light and a cockpit light— that way you'll have a 360 degree white light showing, as required. It's not perfect but it's better than nothing.

Don't turn on your red and green running lights—although many sailors do—unless you are actually underway. It sends a dangerously confusing signal to other vessels.

> **NOTE**: *Some sailors scoff at the anchor ball, thinking it a needless complication. These are sailors who haven't been run into by a rum-sozzled pirate in the middle of the day. The lack of an anchor ball might well void any insurance claim.*

ANCHORING ETIQUETTE:

The first boat in an anchorage sets the style for all other arrivals. If the first one decides to anchor close to shore and put a stern line onto the beach so as not to swing, then all others anchoring close by are expected to do likewise.

If that first boat decides to swing freely to a single anchor, then the next boat can't decide to anchor bow and stern and thus impede boat #1. It's not a law of the sea, but it's definitely the rule of the anchorage. Unless, of course, boat #1 is a 20-foot weekender and boat #2 is a 60-foot motor yacht. Then the Law of Tonnage applies. Woe betide anyone who disregards it!

The best advice is to get to your anchorage early in the afternoon so you have ample time to pick your spot and to check your anchor by snorkeling over it to ensure it is set.

When the new arrival is too close for your comfort, there is the makings of a delicate situation. On one hand, you don't want to be a total *Asterisk* by loudly demanding their immediate departure. On the other, it's not as if he's parked too

close at the mall and you have to squirm your way out of the driver's seat—the danger is he might drag down on you in a 40-knot squall and break some stanchions, if not pull out your anchor with his.

If you are concerned about the way your new neighbor is anchoring, convey that information as quickly and clearly—and gently—as possible. Why let him drop an anchor, lay out chain and go through all the rituals that anchoring demands and then have you announce,

'I say, aren't you a tad too close, Sir?'

No—stand up and wave him away at first opportunity, though with sensitivity of course.

Anchoring in a tight corner, we once had a French voyager shout passionately, 'I have 100 meters of chain. 100 METERS! I swing you all night!'

Not wishing to be swung all night by a florid Frenchman, we moved away. (Though if he really did have 100 meters out, had he swung to port he'd be 20 meters up the beach, and on the other swing he'd be stuck on the reef, but never mind.)

———————

THINGS NEEDN'T BE SO confrontational, however. Follow these steps if a boat motors up to you while you're relaxing in the shady cockpit on your own securely anchored boat. They signify escalating concern:

- Look up from your coffee/tea/beverage
- Give helmsperson a hard stare (as in don't even think about it).
- Stand up with hard stare.
- Walk to a point on your deck closest to offending boat (still with hard stare).
- Fold arms (elevate hard stare to Evil Eye)
- Place hands on your hips (arms akimbo).
- Nothing need be said until this stage is reached. Most newbie bareboaters (even newbie boat owners) are unsure of their anchoring skills and will be looking nervously around at every boat close to them.

Often, the new arrival is so concerned about their anchoring procedures that they don't take enough notice of the neighbors—things may seem settled at that moment but how will it be if a squall rolls through and spins all the boats 90 degrees?

Most will get the idea that they're too close by Step 3 and will decide to move further away. If they persist in anchoring too close (by your definition—not theirs) then resist getting into a shouting match.

Instead, dinghy yourself over and politely point out that you're uncomfortable with their position as it's too close. All but the most belligerent sailor will reluctantly agree and move further off. You could even offer to help them based on your own newfound exper-tise—and so make a new friend!

If another boat does anchor close to you and the skipper shows no interest in honoring your entreaties, no matter how subtle or broad, sometimes the only option is to move away yourself. If this looks like being the case, put all your fenders on the vulnerable side.

Or at the last resort, plan your move carefully since the anchorage is no doubt filling up.

Don't leave it too late. If you are not able to move, deploy your fenders all around the vessel in case your neighbors end up dragging in the night. If you are truly concerned about weather and drag-ging, set an anchor watch overnight—schedule crew on a rotating 3-hour watch from 2100 until sunrise.

OR, if the situation requires drastic action, stand at the rail and bellow, 'I have 100 meters of chain. 100 METERS. I swing you all night.' Accent optional.

It's rather effective.

18

TIE ONE OFF
STERN LINES

I n some anchorages—particularly crowded ones prone to varying changes of wind direction resulting from the local topography—it can make sense to anchor with the vessel's stern close to the shore to keep boats from bumping into each other as they swing in the swirling breeze. Often you'll find that the water depth just a boat length from shore might be 10 feet or more. It is often possible to get within a few feet of the shore and still be in a safe depth (and remember the tidal movement in the Caribbean may be only two feet, maximum).

It is not uncommon to see several yachts lined up next to each other, sterns tied off to trees or rocks on the shore. And remember that it is the first boat to anchor that sets the rule for the anchorage—you won't make any friends if you decide to sit swinging to anchor if you're in the middle of a group of boats anchored fore-and-aft, or with a stern line running ashore. Similarly, if the others are swinging on anchors, don't feel you can drop your hook in the middle of them and set a line ashore—eventually those boats are going to swing into you.

After first checking the chart, your chartplotter and, especially, the cruising guide, one way to verify the suitability is to motor gently towards the shoreline, bow first. Set a hawk-eyed person on the bow to observe the seabed and look for hazards. As you approach, take note of the depths as displayed on your instruments. Once satisfied where the limits of safe water might be, back out and find an appropriate spot to anchor so that the anchor is far enough--has enough scope--out that it'll dig in. But not so far that you'll run out of cable before your stern gets close to the shore.

Once you are satisfied that the anchor is well-set, use two, three, or four dock lines tied together to make up a long-enough stern line. Bareboats don't come with long sets of line for this purpose. Avoid using the kedge anchor warp, as it's often spliced to 15' of chain—and you still might need it as an auxiliary.

You could use the dinghy to get the line ashore, or, if you have a reasonably good swimmer on board, just tie the stern line around their waist and have them swim it to the beach. Once the swimmer is far enough clear of the sterns of the vessel, apply gentle reverse thrust against your anchor to keep the sterns close to shore whilst paying out the stern line to your swimmer.

Be very careful to have the crew member responsible for paying out the line to keep that line clear of the props! And have that person sit down or otherwise brace themselves in case you goose the throttles a tad too much. Little blips of forward or reverse are all that's required. And bear in mind that there's usually a very slight lag between your throttle movements and the props' responding rotation.

Sometimes it will help the swimmer if they attach a fender or other float to the line's midpoint. The seabed can shelve up steeply just a few yards from shore. The assemblage of nylon dock lines will sink to the bottom. The extra weight of line in the water will make the swimmer's task harder than it need be. Adding the float will keep the line on the surface, lessening its drag.

When your swimmer is ashore, have them tie the line around a sturdy rock or tree trunk, making sure it is free of obstructions. When we say *rock* we mean a big, thick substantial rock, not something you might be able to lift an inch off the ground by yourself. And by tree trunk we mean something too thick to be bent by a single person—or even a couple of people.

When tying the line around the rock or tree, the knot to use is the Round Turn and Two Half-Hitches. Why? Because you can untie it even under heavy strain. Unlike, say, the bowline.

With the stern line(s) pulled back and made fast to your stern cleats tighten them by pulling yourself forward a bit, using your anchor windlass.

If staying overnight and if there are other boats close, you will need a second stern line to prevent you from moving sideways and consequently too close to a neighboring vessel in eddying winds and tidal flow changes. In tight quarters, cross the stern lines in an X shape to further stabilize the vessel. Look at how your nearest neighbor has rigged their stern lines and do likewise.

WHEN YOU'RE ready to go, first let out a little anchor chain from the bow. This will give you slack in the system sufficient to make loosening and then untying the shore lines a simple affair. Send someone ashore to release the lines from the tree or rock to which they've been attached. Use the final shore line to pull the crew back to the boat.

If there are still boats similarly anchored close to you, keep from drifting into them by using your engine in low reverse gear to stretch out the anchor cable. In stiff cross winds, you'll need to quickly reel yourself forward to get out of the way. And, of course, have the crew brace themselves for unexpected movement as they carefully tend to the lines. Go easy on the throttles--those engines and their props are powerful!

While this may seem a complicated business, it is really fairly simple. After having done it a couple of times, you'll be able to get the boat tied down quickly. You'll find you have created a great platform for swimming in the shallows, walking on the beach, and other pleasures that are a little more complicated when swinging at anchor.

19

PICKUP ARTISTRY
PLAY BALL

Showtime!

The mooring field is one of the two main theaters where:
Sometimes you watch the show, or

Sometimes you are the show.

B efore you get to enjoy watching the show from the comfort of your catamaran's comfortable lounges, you and your crew will have already performed for the audience that got there ahead of you. So be sure to give them a good show (and by that, we mean showing the crowd how picking up a mooring should be done).

When picking up a mooring, the thing to keep in mind is our motto: *Slow is Pro.*

HERE'S HOW

Moorings in the Caribbean consist of mainly two types,

1. Proper Mooring balls, and

2. The Rest—Free-floating lines with a float attached, such as a bleach bottle or a detergent jug.

PROPER MOORING BALLS are associated with the better-managed anchorages. These are moorings in which lines or cable are professionally laid. A chain or robust line leads from a sturdy sand screw or large concrete block up to a large plastic floating ball. You pay for them but you'll get a receipt from a real company and the knowledge that there's someone to go after in the unlikely event the mooring fails.

The Rest are none of the above.

Choose Wisely!

———————

THE LINES or cable attached to a proper mooring ball are of two types:

1. *The downline*: Rope or chain which drops vertically to the seabed from the floating plastic ball. This chain is attached to a concrete block or an eye drilled into the rock or screwed into the sand, and

2. *The pennant (or pendant)*: This is attached to the downline at the fitting on the floating plastic ball and floats free on the water, waiting to be picked up and attached to a cleat aboard ship. Often, the pennant will have a small plastic float attached to keep the eye floating on the surface, so aim to hook the pennant and not the float.

This eye is at the free end of the pennant and usually has a plastic or metal fitting within it. This fitting makes it difficult to simply slip the eye over a cleat, so please don't try.

. . .

THE PROPER WAY TO attach the mooring pennant is

1. By attaching a line (almost always a dock line) to a cleat
   and leading it, clear of all obstructions, to the pennant.
2. Then passing it through the eye and leading it back to the
   cleat it started from, so both ends of the line are attached to
   the same cleat.
3. The line can be first attached by tying a bowline in one end
   and passing the loop of that knot through the base of the
   cleat and over the horns.
4. If the base is too narrow and can't accommodate the loop
   being pushed through, just tie a bowline through the base
   and cleat-hitch the returning end.
5. Or, simply attach the line by way of a cleat hitch, then lead
   it through the eye of the mooring pennant, then back to
   the cleat—where you can tie another cleat hitch atop the
   first.

Do the same on the opposite side, so you have two looped lines. One running starboard-starboard and the other port-port.

Simply leading a single line from port to starboard will allow the vessel to slide along its length creating chafe and causing wide swings in gusty weather.

ON SOME CATS, the mooring lines are led from cleats attached to the cross beam at the bows. On others, they are led from cleats on the outside of each hull. Yet other models have special cleats attached to the inside edge of each hull. Make sure your deck crew inspect the yacht and check with your boat briefer to see which applies to you.

WHEN APPROACHING THE MOORING BALL, these port and starboard lines should each already be attached at one end, with the free end led first outside the vessel beneath the deck railings, then laid back over the same railings in readiness. Much depends on the wind conditions. In calm weather with a small breeze, it is a simple thing for the person driving the boat to motor up to place the mooring at the feet of the line handler.

Foredeck Crew Guides the Approach to the Mooring

Charter catamarans come with a vast array of differing helm positions, so hand signals from one person on the foredeck may be essential to confirm the skipper's view.

At the crew's signal, the driver should apply a gentle burst of reverse to bring the vessel to a stop. The crew member can simply lean over and pluck the pennant from the surface with a boathook.

Mooring lines led around outside of hull

BY USING THE THROTTLES CAREFULLY, the driver can hold position while the deck crew thread the dock lines through the eye of the pennant and back to the appropriate cleats, either attached to the cross-beam or to the outside of each hull.

LOOK 90 degrees left or right to find a transit and make sure the boat is holding position so the line handlers can work their magic efficiently.

Two crew can work together and secure each line simultaneously. If you have only one able-bodied person to handle the lines, have them snug-up the first bridle as tightly as they can and temporarily cleat it off while they thread through the other one. At this stage, the driver can come forward and take out the slack on the second line as the crew working the bow position surges out the first until they're equal.

If you've got a reasonably able crew (of any age) you can easily teach them to thread the second line straight after the first and then lead them back together while the driver keeps the boat hovering on the spot.

In some extreme situations—inclement weather, missing boat hook —the smart thing might be to put your dinghy into the water and motor it around to the bow and pass up the pennant by hand!

> **NOTE:** *If you have been shown a different method by an experienced teacher on a different type of boat, and it still works for you on a big catamaran, by all means use it. There are so many variables in terms of freeboard and cleat placement among the various brands and sizes of charter cats—and they are changing constantly—that we will just stay with the tried and true.*

One habit of mooring balls is that when the wind drops, or local tide current changes, they sometimes tap against the hull, making an annoying sound for occupants of the forward cabins. Stop this by hauling on the mooring pennant so the ball is pulled clear of the water—it's the small chop and water movement caused by the change of tide or the wake of a passing dinghy that creates the tapping sound, so pulling the ball up removes it from these influences.

Remove the mooring line from the bridle and pull as tight as possible to prevent tapping against the hull.

If you forget to do this and get woken up in the night, just put in some earplugs or earbuds because by then there's nothing you can do about it and no harm will be done to the boat.

A simple way to check the health of the mooring line is to grab a face mask and fins and jump in the water. Follow the mooring line down to see that all parts are secure. The places to check are the shackles both beneath the mooring ball and at the bottom of the downline where it meets the sand screw or concrete block (watch for unsecured shackle screw pins), the top end of the downline (in case some cowboy has wrapped the line around their propeller).

To stop the ball tapping on the hulls, haul the line tight.

SUCH ISSUES ARE rare these days but, in the (approximate) words of the great Captain Ron: *"If it's going to happen, it'll happen out there."*

The most likely time to find these anomalies is at the end of the busy charter season when the moorings have been given a stressful months-long workout. If you have any doubts, try for a better mooring. Check most thoroughly in those favorite snorkel spots that attract hundreds of boats per week and are a must-stop on everyone's itinerary.

RECENTLY, some BVI destinations, such as Norman Island, have installed mooring balls where previously there had been none— Benures Bay, for example. This serves a two-fold purpose:

- It frees up the congested bays where anchoring is difficult (because of the water depth) but demand for the available moorings is high, and

- It allows sailors who aren't confident in their anchoring skills to enjoy the anchorages which were previously unavailable. And bear in mind that while a charter skipper might be quite capable of anchoring a boat, they may be nervous about doing so in extremely tight circumstances—preferring a mooring for the peace of mind it can offer.

These private balls are for advanced bookings only

And, in the BVI as well, since 2017 a company called BoatyBall has made it possible to reserve certain mooring balls in advance via a dedicated app.

20

DOCK APPROACHES
SLIP TIPS

No charter company will let you take out one of their Power Cats unless you've had some prior boat-handling experience. But that experience often isn't on another PC. Even if you've chartered a sailing catamaran before—or a heavy trawler-style power vessel—judging speed, distance, and the actions of other boat operators is a skill that can be developed with experience and time, but you probably don't have a lot of either in a vessel of this length and breadth, with this type of engine.

NOTE: *The only way to truly perfect your docking technique is the same as with anything else: practice makes perfect.*

Even a little practice in a quiet corner of a bay or harbor will improve your skills immensely. Experienced skippers on a new type of boat for the first time will often spend an hour maneuvering around a line of mooring balls, doing Figure-8s forward and back, checking to see how quickly the vessel responds to the throttles, the movement of the throttles, how quickly the boat will stop when in reverse, what kind of sound the engine makes at various RPMs and so forth. Later, when doing the maneuvers for real, the results should be more predictable.

Before beginning any dock-approach maneuvers, be aware that there might be one or more casual observers standing on the dock—perhaps waiting for a friend to pick them up in a dinghy, perhaps just wandering the marina to look at the pretty boats. They will be instantly attracted to your approaching vessel—finally, some action!

Pay them no mind. Keep your attention confined to your boat and others that might get in its way, the wind, the dock, the targets on the dock, and other items. Any distractions from bystanders—who may know something about what you are doing, but often have no clue at all—will be to the detriment of your work. So go ahead and keep your attention to things that directly impact your performance. Though if a bystander shouts, "There's a puppy in the water," you might pay heed!

DOCKING: Here are the two main categories of things to think about when docking. Some you can control or at least be aware of and be able to factor into your decision-making. Others are factors beyond your control that you have to learn to work with or live with.

THINGS YOU CAN CONTROL:

Rate of Turn: On all boats, you can judge the rate of turn by seeing how quickly your boat's bow moves against the background. Use one of the boat's forward-most guardrail stanchions (posts) as a reference.

On a PC it's often difficult—or impossible—to see all four corners from your helm station, so appoint a spotter and ask them for feedback as to distance off the dock, other boats, dinghies in the water, etc. (Plate 1)

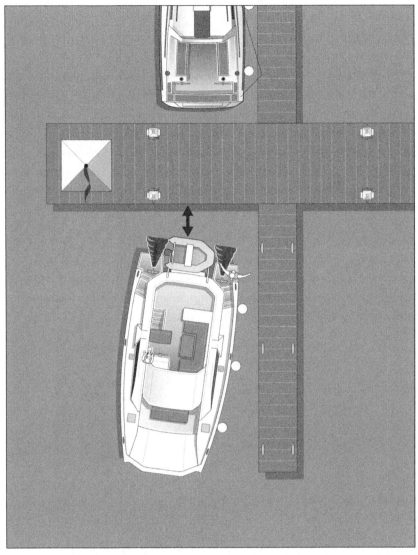

1) Appoint a spotter to help guide you in

You can make it a little easier on yourself by docking the boat on the same side as your helm station. On some boats that station is to port, on others to starboard.

. . .

ARC OF TURN: When turning while going forward, try to focus not only on the movement of the bow. Don't forget that the stern is moving sideways, but in the opposite direction. The resultant arc is also affected by the fact that you are in a fluid and that the boat slides or crabs as it turns, like a car skidding sideways through a turn. Be aware that, going forward, the stern of one hull is on the outside of your turning circle while the bow of the opposite hull is on the inside. It's the opposite going stern-first. In both cases, it's the pivot point of the boat that actually defines the circumference of your turning circle—and that pivot point moves left to right of the centerline as you vary the thrust.

Once you're in close quarters maneuvering mode—less than 1.5 - 2 knots, or modest walking speed—the wheel will be centered and you'll be using only your engines. Once stopped, by using roughly equal opposing thrust on both engines, you'll be able to spin a cat around in just over a boat length. (Plate 2)

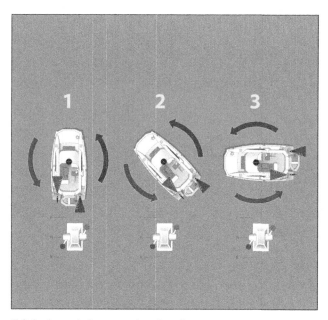

2) Spin the cat in just over a boat length

Glide Zone: This is how far momentum will carry the boat forward or backward without any engine thrust. It will vary greatly depending on wind speed and direction—as well as your boat's own size, weight and speed when you engage neutral—as well as the cleanliness of the hulls!

Blades: In most of the Power Cats in the bareboat fleets, the rudder is aft of the propeller, in the usual way. There are other types of propulsion arrangements with rotating pods and forward facing propellers but they are not found in charter fleets--yet. When you engage forward gear, a flow of water from the propeller immediately rushes over the leading edge of your rudder that, unless the steering wheel is locked, will simply align itself with the flow.

If, however, the props on your PC are behind the rudders, no flow passes over the rudders in forward gear. In reverse, though, a rush of water is forced against the trailing edge of your rudder. Because the rudder posts are all closer to the rudders' leading edge, your rudders will slam against their stops to the right or left, unless the wheel is locked or held firm. These full-left or full-right rudders will not help your backward maneuvering in close quarters, and could suffer damage.

But, whatever sort of PC you're on, center the wheel and leave it alone in all close quarter, slow speed maneuvering.

THE DOCK LINE OF APPROACH:

Reconnoiter the dock. Are there any dock staff? Call on your VHF to ask permission or guidance from the dockmaster, particularly if picking up fuel or water. Do an initial pass-by to check out the space available. What's the dock height for your fenders? Are there cleats or bollards?

Consider the wind and the available maneuvering space; circle back around to the starting point you've chosen to begin your approach.

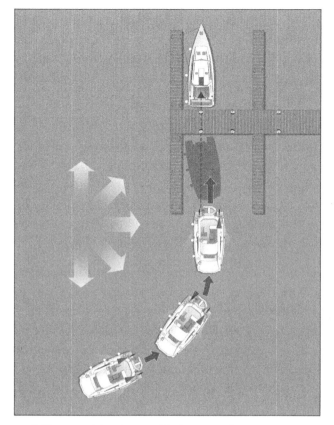

3) Use a transit bearing to guide the approach

Looking at the dock, decide where you'd like the aft end of your boat to be when docked. As a guide to help you drive one of your PC's corners to a target cleat, pick out two vertical objects, one in front of the other—a dock power post or fuel pump in front of a yacht's mast, for example.

As you proceed toward the dock, by keeping these objects in line (a transit) you'll be following the correct line of approach. (Plate 3)

Based on the dock height, set your fenders so that they protect your boat—neither too high nor dragging in the water. All modern Power Cats have portlights on the sides of the hulls so align the fenders to avoid them.

Set fenders to avoid port lights

Cockpit Conversation: Have a docking plan and discuss it thoroughly with everyone before beginning the maneuver. Turn off any music or extraneous sounds aboard your boat. Assign roles—spring line, bow line, stern line, fenders, etc. Agree on hand signals and make sure everyone understands what is required of them. Encourage them to ask questions if there's any doubt or ambiguity. Only then, spread your crew around to their assigned positions. Make sure that you can see each other or the hand signals won't work. If necessary, post an extra person to relay signals from the unseen spotter.

Execute your plan using hand signals rather than voice commands because they won't be able to hear you 30-40 feet (10-12 meters) away and over the noise of the engine, other boats, music from the bar (there's always music), and birds squawking.

THINGS YOU CAN'T CONTROL:

Wind: We live in the air. We feel it around us; we see the effects it has on clouds, water, flags, and trees. It will blow your hat off. We can't control it, but must be aware of it and learn to work with it. Observe wind direction and speed and what the combined effect of these will be on your boat as you approach the dock—and when you've come to a stop alongside.

Check your cockpit indicator for wind direction at the boat and the courtesy and other high flags on boats that are already at the dock. The wind may be entirely different in your location if you're 50 yards/meters out. And it may be different at deck level than higher up. Watch for sudden changes in intensity and direction—gusts, lulls—as you come in. Docks and buildings can create wind eddies and shadows. Some docks are more exposed to the prevailing trade winds.

Docking at them with a moderate to fresh wind is like parking a car on a steep hill: if you're approaching downwind (down the hill) you'll need very little—If any—power, as the wind will push you. As always on a catamaran, check that the wind isn't pushing you sideways or off your desired line.

If you're approaching upwind, (uphill) you'll need more—possibly constant—low power to keep moving against it.

CURRENT: Current is minimal in most Caribbean docking situations. The oceanic current is slight and most docks are situated in protected harbors.

> **NOTE**: *If you do find that you have some current where you're docking, be aware that water is 800 times denser than air, so just one knot of current is equivalent to about 10-15 knots of wind speed from the same direction.*

Also, watch out for ferries and other boats at the dock that may be tied up but have their engines running and props turning—they can put out a stream of water more powerful than any current.

OTHER BOATS: They were here before you, so you just have to work around or in between them. If you can't stem the wind directly, be careful of getting blown sideways on to the boats to leeward of your chosen line of approach.

Close to the dock, look for activity on the deck of boats there—people getting lines ready, someone at the helm. A vessel might be about to leave and so make your approach easier—don't be afraid to swing by and ask them.

Check Your Six: And always look behind you. There's no rearview mirror (though there may be a rear-facing camera). Someone may be following you in.

HELPFUL HANGABOUTS: Boat folks are generally a friendly and helpful bunch and will happily put down their beverage to assist another sailor. They do the same for each other, too—it's not that you're an obvious newbie, it's that almost everyone could use a hand. But there is a type of helpful hangabout who is not like these kind folk. You'll encounter them when you come into a dock and the dockhands are busy or on a break and there are no working mariners around.

They're the well-intentioned, clueless stranger who might be a first-time bareboater, a charter guest, or some tourist just walking along the dock to look at the boats—a doofus on a daytrip.

These people might be fine human beings who just want to help—but can they handle a line, tie a hitch, or know a cleat from a clarinet? If you have a plan and are confident that you can execute it, you can politely wave away their proffered assistance and say something like, "No thanks. Practicing!"

We've seen well-intentioned dock walkers do the craziest things with dock lines. And bear in mind that you can say the same thing to the dock guys, the professional crew, or the Admiral of the Fleet. They'll understand. But you'd better pull it off!

And bear in mind, too, that most dockhands have seen every imaginable docking variable. They are well prepared, so listen to what they say. If you can't hear the dock guys or are not sure of what they're saying, don't just ignore them. Use the phrase "Say again," if you want them to repeat something.

And give them plenty of time, since there are a myriad of calls on their attention: Guests wanting ice or fuel, departing boats, garbage pickups and the like. If you can be patient, the dock guys will be most appreciative. But be ready with your lines in place, fenders attached, your crew dispersed as necessary. That way the dockhands will be able to concentrate on the essentials.

21

CAT TRICKS
PUT IT WHERE YOU WANT IT

O ne of the joys of operating a modern Power Cat is how easy it is to drive and to dock.

Although at first glance it looks like you're driving something approaching the size of a squash court, docking a catamaran is a much easier skill to learn and execute than docking a similarly sized power monohull.

CATAMARAN DOCKING ADVANTAGES INCLUDE:

- Widely spaced propellers driven by efficient modern diesel engines coupled with propellers that give a powerful grip in the water. This efficiency means you shouldn't need high RPMs on your engines.
- Shallow keels and small rudders, so there's not much underwater profile to create resistance.
- An elevated helm station giving a commanding view. The position of the helm varies according to make and model, but in general the control position is high and open on all sides. The operator can cross from one side to the other

with a few steps to gauge distance off the dock, check the stern for clearance when tying off in a slip, or just get a sense of the layout in and around the docking position.

- Many larger PCs come equipped with video cameras viewable on the MFD screens at the helm so the aft view can be monitored when backing down. A PC of less than 40 feet LOA may have a central driving position with a clear view over the aft deck below.

- A pivot point that you control because it changes as you change engine thrust. It moves fore-and-aft/side-to-side as you adjust throttle pressure. It's on the centerline at the centerpoint when equal thrust is applied fore and aft on each propeller.

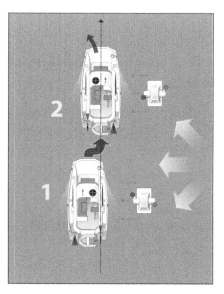

4) Observe the pivot point move to the side with least thrust

- But it shifts toward the side generating the least thrust as you change throttle position. And when docking you can further change the pivot point with a dock line attached to the vessel at bow, stern or mid-ships. (Plate 4)

These advantages can make your arrivals on, and departures from the dock less stressful and you will maximize your ability to hover—that is, hold position while you decide what to do next. And should you need to bail out of a maneuver you'll do so confidently and under control.

THERE ARE, however, a few complications inherent in the design of the cruising cat that can impact these close-quarter maneuvers:

- Sightlines: As noted above, every model is different in layout. While they all do well when under way and the sightlines are long, when approaching a dock there will always be blind spots. It's just as well you have crew aboard to feed you information as you get close to the concrete.
- Small rudders that are ineffective under about 1.5 – 2 knots.
- The same shallow keels and small rudders also offer less resistance to the effects of wind. This relative imbalance of windage to underwater resistance means the boat can more easily get blown to leeward in a breeze.
- Freeboard. Side decks are high. Apart from creating more windage, they also make stepping onto the dock from the boat more difficult.

BACKING UP: Driving a cat in reverse is much easier than with a single-screw powerboat—even one with a variable-thrust outboard or outdrive because the props are so widely spaced, and the lateral resistance of the two hulls eliminates prop walk. Also, even though one of the two sterns may be out of your sightline, the other will be close to the helm. Work off this side and you'll easily judge distance-off and speed of approach. Station someone to signal distance-off anything hidden behind a blind spot. Agree upon signals with the crew as discussed in Ch. 11.

Since you're likely to have only one helm station with engine controls, try to dock that-side-to unless you absolutely can't—at least until you get used to the boat. With practice, you'll be able to dock on either side as easily as you can park your car either side to a curb. But make it easy on yourself initially.

If you do choose—or must—dock on the offside hull, be aware that you are operating the boat from a position far away from the dock. So you must position a spotter at that side to give you precise information as to what is happening in places you can't see, or see well.

> **NOTE**: *If at all possible, when driving astern position yourself so that you're facing in the direction of travel. On some Power Cats, you can stand, crouch or sit forward or to the side of the Dual Lever controls—these have the gearshift and throttle functions for each engine combined into a single lever for each engine. You'll be able to see where you're going without looking over your shoulder, as you might in your car.*

Some PCs feature an aft-facing camera that can give you a picture of your otherwise concealed corner—it'll be a page on your multifunction chartplotter display. Just as when parking your car at the mall, you have to keep your eyes open to everything around you, and not get mesmerised by the screen. Even if you have it, it may not work. And it's not something that you want to get reliant on.

> **NOTE**: *There is a concept in naval operations called the* Radar-Assisted Collision. *We try to avoid them. You should, too. (It applies to more than just the radar!)*

Because of freeboard and sightline advantages, we recommend backing down stern-first as close to parallel to the dock as you can. Ideally, you will be able to position your aft cleat closest to the target dockside cleat or bollard. Get your line to the dock by passing the line to a waiting dockhand, or by throwing a bight (open loop) from the boat around the dock cleat or bollard, and bring the line back to the shipboard cleat.

This lassoing from the sugar-scoop stern of a cat will be a lot easier as these steps are lower and closer to the cleat.

To make it even easier, open the gate or lifelines guarding the aft steps to simplify throwing a bight around the cleat. Do not let your crew step off the boat. If they miss the first throw, hold the boat in place using your engines only, or re-position until they can do it again. They should be prepared for sudden surges of movement if you're accidentally too heavy on the throttles.

Once attached by the stern cleat, motor ahead gently on the 'outside' engine with some counter (reverse) thrust on the 'inside' engine and the boat will swing parallel against the dock.

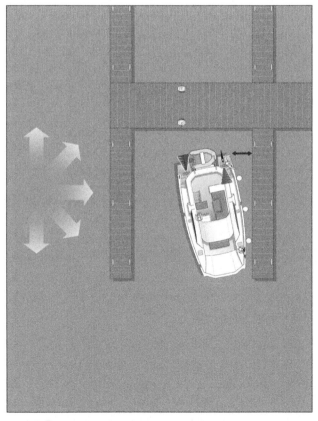

5) Use counter thrust to position the vessel

Maintain this gentle thrust until all remaining docklines are secured. And you're done! (Plate 5)

As mentioned above, *go gently on the throttle*s since your line handlers will have both hands full and won't be holding on to anything to support themselves. An inadvertently enthusiastic move on the throttles could send them flying. If, by mischance a line gets dropped in the water at the stern, put the near-engine into neutral until it's retrieved. And, as with all throttles/shifters, be sure to pause in neutral for a moment before engaging the next gear selection. Most gear selectors emit a short *beep* to let you know when you've found *Neutral*.

As said previously, but it bears repeating—When maneuvering at low speed, you'll find that the rudders are ineffective at less than 1.5 - 2 knots. So before you get close to the dock, center the wheel—the hydraulic control will keep it there.

HERE's a useful way to think about the relationship between you and your cat's throttle/shifters when you're operating in close proximity to a concrete dock and other expensive boats:

Imagine your catamaran as a big airport/supermarket-style push-cart. Your hands rest on the horizontal push/pull bar. Imagine how you move your hands, elbows, and shoulders as you maneuver your trolley around the aisles of a supermarket or around people in the airport. Let's say you want to turn your trolley to the left 90 degrees, but without going forward. You'd push forward with your right hand and pull back with your left.

How much you pull and push depends on how heavy your trolley is and how strong you are. You may be better at pushing than pulling—just like most propellers are more efficient at going forward than in reverse. So, in our example above, you compensate by pulling back a tad harder with your left hand to prevent the trolley from advancing forward. You operate your throttles/shifters with differential thrust in exactly the same fashion.

Now, with this analogy in mind, there are two ways to rotate your catamaran:

- One speeds you up (forward or backward) as you turn.
- One turns you without speeding you up.
- Which one you use depends on what you want to achieve and how much room you have to maneuver.
- When docking, space is almost always limited and so we don't want to advance our cat forwards or backwards when we need to rotate.
- By applying one off-center engine in forward gear, your cat will go ahead and rotate away from that force. By applying the other off-center engine in reverse, you can eliminate that forward component to zero and just have the rotation
- As you make your way closer to your final approach, keep speed somewhere between 2 and 4 knots. Just enough so you can steer the boat.
- If your cat is going at the speed and in the direction that you want, let the boat glide with the engines in neutral.
- Use short blips or pulses of power to adjust your heading— usually just to the first indent on the shifter. This indent— which can feel like a little notch in the throttle advancement—isn't all there on some electronic throttles. But the point remains: finesse your final approach by using small short shots of power.
- Alternate the engines so you "walk" the boat forward. You can maintain momentum with less speed this way by using gentle blips of power on one engine, then the other.
- Don't always use forward thrust to adjust your heading because doing so will make you go faster as you turn— which is seldom what you want when close maneuvering. To counter that unwanted speed, try using a blip of reverse

on just one engine in order to re-align yourself to your desired track.

HERE'S HOW:

With your wheel on the centerline, here's how to dock any Power Cat:

- Use engines—as described above—to bring the chosen corner of the vessel to the target cleat or bollard on the dock. Generally one of your stern corners is better—by varying thrust to the near and offside engines you can bring a cat's corner tight into the dock. Be gentle with the electronic throttles—you don't want the boat to surge and apply sudden excess pressure to the dock line
- Using only your throttle/gear shift controls, make your approach to the dock, preferably using a transit—two vertical markers of your choosing.
- Have dock lines attached and ready (bow, stern, and midships) and led properly outside of all impediments, coiled and ready for use. Attach fenders, keeping in mind the height of tide and the type of dock. Many docks have boards all the way down to the sea surface, so a fender sitting a few inches off the water is often in a good position. Otherwise, do a dry run first to eyeball the height of the dock and location of dock cleats or bollards. If in doubt, alternate high and low fenders—you can adjust the incorrect ones when you're safely on the dock. Be careful not to place fenders over the portlights (windows) in the side of your cat—lean over to check, or it could get expensive.
- Assign crew positions and roles. Aside from the driver, you need one person to indicate "distance off", and another with the ability to throw a line over a cleat that should be brought about 6-10 feet away from the thrower's hands.

Practice on the foredeck beforehand. Throw into the boat, not over the water, in order to keep the dock-line dry--they are much lighter to throw that way!

- On your final approach, come in at any angle that you can, using your throttles to compensate for wind—even so far as to approach directly into it if there's a stiff breeze. (Plate 6)
- Stop your desired corner about a foot before touching, (this is hard to judge from the helm station so see the tip list on measuring distance-off).
- Get a single bow or stern line made fast to the dock. Any of your four corners will do, but choose the one with the best sight lines.

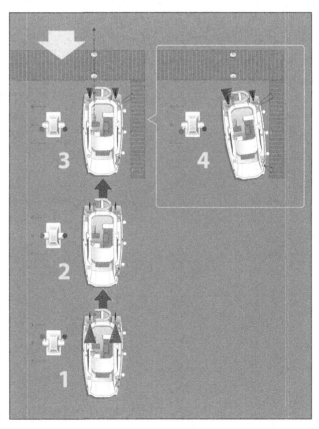

(Plate 6)

- Stern attachments are often best because of the proximity to the driver, lower topsides, detachable lifelines, and use of the sugar scoop as a throwing platform. Make this first line as short as you can but it'll still work when a bit long—just shorten it up later when you can use the engines to relieve the tension on it.
- Once this first line is fixed to the dock, use your outside engine to bring the cat parallel to the dock. Whether you use forward or reverse—or a combination of the two—will depend on which corner the line is attached to.
- Although we use pulses of power when maneuvering to the dock, once you've got that first line secured, apply steady power, gently, to bring your vessel parallel and snug to the dock.
- Once bow and stern lines are shortened-up, set at least one midships spring line to prevent backward or forward movement impacting other craft.

NOTE: *Electronic controls require a very gentle touch because they offer little friction-based resistance to the driver, plus they have a slight time-lag which can cause the operator to be tricked into thinking they need more power—and then find they have added too much.*

22

COWBOY UP

ROPE TRICKS

W hen approaching a dock, without the assistance of any dockhands, the best technique for attaching a dockline to a shoreside cleat or bollard varies depending on the type of boat. The main difference lies in whether it is safer and easier to stay aboard the vessel than to step off onto the dock.

As cruising yachts of all types have increased in size in recent years —not overall length necessarily, but interior volume definitely—free-board has increased as well.

So, what used to be an easy step down from the deck to the dock is now often a heart-stopping leap, accompanied by the risk of a twisted ankle or knee, the dropping of the line or a staggering waltz around the (inevitable) group of bemused bystanders. So what's the alternative?

The best option is to stay aboard the vessel and throw (or drop) a loop of line—a bight—from the deck down to and around the dock-side cleat or bollard, then to secure the free end back on deck, around the originating cleat. The method—the Operatic method— for throwing the line is often described as throwing a Lasso, though it differs from the cowboy version in that the loop that is thrown is an open loop (the bunch of line between the two ends) and not a closed one.

HERE'S HOW:

First, if your boat has docklines with a pre-spliced or pre-made loop in one end, slide it through-and-over the cleat (from the outside). If not, make a bowline and do the same. This trick frees up space on the the horns of the cleat where the end of this dock line will ultimately be secured.

- Having thus attached the ends of the docklines to the cleats on board your vessel—at bow, stern, and midships—coil each line toward the remaining working end, making several loops of a full arms length apart and each made with a half-roll away from you to remove any twist in the line.
- Divide these assembled loops neatly in two so that half of them are in one hand, and half in the other.
- Make sure the line is free to run and not entangled in railings or other metalwork. There are two ways of casting off your loops. If you're the line thrower, your choice will depend on how close the driver can bring the boat to the target cleat, and your height and arm strength.

THE BACKSWING METHOD:

Let's say that your driver is being very cautious, or hasn't been able to bring you as close to your target as you'd like.

7) The Backswing Method

Provided you're no further than about ten feet (3 meters) away you can still get your bight home by standing somewhat sideways (inboard or outboard depending if you're right or left-handed) and employing a backswing to both sets of loops. (Plate 7)

Do two or three swings to establish a rhythm. But make sure that no railings are in the way of your swing.

THE OPERATIC METHOD:

This is for shorter throws, where the line-thrower is within six feet of the target. Here, the loops in the other hand should be held loosely as well, with palms facing inward—toward your chest.

8) Think of a tenor at the end of the opera

Now bring both the hands, with the loops of line held securely, together at chest level, just touching the sternum. Then fling both hands out wide, releasing the loops of line when your arms are fully extended. Think of a tenor throwing out his arms at the end of a performance. (Plate 8)

> **NOTE**: *Never aim at your target cleat or bollard—unless your target is right at the corner of a dock— always aim beyond it and then pull the boat end back to snare your target. You'll probably surprise yourself and get it right first time.*

IMPORTANT: In both methods, the loops of line are released at the end of the front swing as the arms reach their full extension so that all is released. But the line is **still firmly grasped at the end by the fingers of the releasing hand**. Just before you make your final approach, try to practice by making a few dummy throws inboard into your boat to keep the line dry— you'll be surprised how far you can cast! This way, you'll throw with greater confidence of your range.

THE THROWER MUST NOW SMARTLY GATHER the line back aboard the vessel, and having made it as short as possible, quickly make it fast around the cleat it started from in the usual fashion, creating a tight loop around the dockside target—the shorter, the better. But they need to get it on as fast as they can, since the driver can't perform his next maneuver until they do. If on a vessel where the driver can't see clearly, have someone relay by voice or, better, hand signal (a 'thumbs-up') that the line is made.

The remaining corner and spring lines are leisurely lassoed in the same way while the boat is pinned securely to the dock by the appropriate gentle engine thrust. The boat, now secured, can be left with the lines exactly as-is for a short time while refueling or shopping. For a longer stay, they should be retied ship-style with the standing end on the dock and the working end together with the rest of the line attached to the boat's cleats and neatly coiled on deck.

If the thrown line doesn't initially loop properly around the dockside cleat, it can be pulled back aboard and re-thrown as described above. This is where the driver's hovering skills come into play so that the throw can be repeated several times—even if it means maneuvering the boat away from the dock and returning to position it as close as desired. In this way, everyone stays on the boat and there are no crew left waiting on the dock.

23

BEACH BUGGY
THE DINGHY

The dink, the RIB, the Zodiac, the skiff—the yacht's inflatable dinghy has many names and many purposes. The cheery nicknames indicate just how important the little boat is to the charter. It can serve as a workhorse, or a "funabout" taking the kids on joyrides (keeping safe distance from the neighbors, of course!). But whatever you call it, and however you use it, you need to keep it in good order.

On a Power Cat, it should always be in davits when you are underway. Secure it well so it doesn't swing back and forth and chafe against the davit supports. Attach lines to the U-bolt in the dinghy's bow and to one of the stern U-bolts, if there are any. Secure these lines to the aft shipboard cleats. If your dinghy doesn't have U-bolts or pad eyes for this purpose, ask your boat briefer how best to secure it. There are many creative ways of achieving this—often using the tail end of the davit lines around the leg of the outboard engine. Always remove the bung/drain stopper when underway—and secure it to the dinghy with a length of small line. If you are traveling a very short distance, it is possible to tow the little boat but you'll need someone to attend to the dinghy painter so it doesn't foul your prop. The powered davits on your PC are easy to use, so there's really no reason to take this risk and unnecessary worry.

Keep the dinghy on a long line, well free of the dock

Underway, a heavy squall will fill the dinghy with unwanted weight, so whenever the dink is in the davits, pull the plug if there's any danger of rain—and remember to put it back in before you next launch it.

When on a mooring or at anchor, bail out rain water from your dinghy by hoisting it in the davits just clear of the sea surface and letting the water flow out of the open drain hole. Be sure to replace the bung before releasing your securing lines and dropping the dink back into the water.

When starting the outboard via a pull cord, you can avoid the common problem of bashing people in the head as you pull the cord by ensuring that you are the only person in the dinghy when you start it. Only after you have it running to your satisfaction should the rest of the gang join you.

SOME EASY FIXES FOR COMMON PROBLEMS:

- Before starting, check that the air vent on top of the fuel tank is in the open position. If not, the engine will start and run but will soon quit after about 30 seconds.
- The bulb in the fuel line lets you prime the pump— gently squeeze the bulb until it feels firm.

- Watch that the fuel line doesn't get pinched by the tank lying on top of it. Or by your foot, for that matter.
- If you pull too many times on the outboard's start cord and it fails to start, you've likely flooded it with gas—you can probably smell it, too. To get it going again, disconnect the quick-release fuel line from the engine, close the choke and pull again with the throttle wide open (max revs). With that wet fuel now evaporated, It'll likely fire up straight away. Quickly bring down the revs and reconnect the fuel line.
- Whether you're right or left-handed, the dinghy is designed for the operator to sit on the starboard-side tube and steer with the left hand because the tiller arm, gear shift, and throttle twist rotation are all optimized for this operation.
- Have the person sitting farthest in front hold the painter when underway in daylight, and the painter and a flashlight when underway at night, keeping a lookout for unlit boats and mooring balls.
- Don't tie-up too tight to the dock—leave room for others to come in. In a busy area, it's a good idea to leave plenty of painter—a full dinghy length off the dock—so other boaters can fit. Either coil your remaining painter tidily on the dock or, if there's a lot left over, throw it back in your dinghy and not leave it as trip hazard on the dock.
- If you have a choice, tie up on the leeward side of the dinghy dock. If there is any chop or swell running, use the dink's anchor, attached to the stern, to hold it away from—and keep it from smashing against—the dock while you're away. Or, even worse, getting crushed beneath it.
- **Always** leave the motor in the down position—otherwise you risk having the propeller bashed by a moving dink or of damaging someone else's dinghy.
- These days, most PCs have electric or propane barbecues. But if you are operating a charcoal-fired BBQ, keep the dinghy well clear (if it's in the water) by tying it off to a midships cleat, well forward of the stern. If the dinghy is in

davits, keep a wet towel or a full bucket of seawater close by to smother any stray sparks.

- Beaching the dinghy in surf is generally frowned upon by every charter company—if not specifically forbidden. Surging swell and breaking waves are too great to risk— even if all is calm when you head off to the restaurant, by the time you get back it could be entirely different. Dinghies can get tossed around, have their anchors torn out or be filled with sand and seawater by just a few unfortunate swells.

- Dinghy painters are one of the most common causes of fouled propellers and drive shafts—especially on catamarans with their shallow props, so be extra careful when reversing with a dinghy under tow.

- Beach excursions will bring sand into the dinghy. Shake off as much as you can before you get in. Once in, dunk sandy legs over the side of the dinghy in order to rinse it off.

- Once the dinghy's back to the mother ship and raised in the davits, throw a few buckets of sea water in to flush sand out of the opened plughole. And have a bucket of seawater ready to dip those sandy feet into as soon as you get on the mother ship and before you proceed further.

- Let no one step off the aft deck until they have thoroughly cleaned their feet and legs of grains of sand. Keep sandy shoes isolated from the rest of the boat.

- Even better, have everyone slip out of the dinghy and swim to the ship's ladder, making sure to flush the sand from swim suits and every nook and cranny while in the water. And make sure the dinghy engine is not running!

Dinghy light. Your charter company should provide you with the legally required white all-round light. Most don't, but supply a flash-light/torch instead—which is good enough. Make sure that you take it with you when you leave if you're planning on coming back to the boat after sunset. Lots of excited bareboaters forget it when they leave for Happy Hour in bright sunshine at 1700 and are surprised when it's dark at 1830. As a last resort, turn on your phone (safely within its dry pouch) and let the light shine outwards. You don't really need the light for illumination—though make sure you don't run over a mooring ball—you need the light so others can see you.

The Kill Cord: Every dinghy comes equipped with a small plastic clip that slips over a spring-powered pull out knob. To start the outboard, this clip must be attached behind the pulled out knob to prevent it from breaking the circuit and stopping the motor from running. This clip is attached to a plastic lanyard which should be wrapped around the boat operator's wrist (or ankle) whenever the motor is running. If the dinghy runs aground, a passenger slips overboard, the boat hits a rock, is swamped by another vessel's wake or any of a number of dangers should occur, the operator has only to jerk their arm or leg and the clip will pull out of the knob and the motor will instantly stop running.

Not everyone does this, since it seems to be an inconvenience but terrible things can happen in a dinghy—particularly where there has been alcohol consumed—not necessarily by the crew on your boat, of course.

It's the Caribbean. There's rum involved. Be careful out there.

24

LOCK 'ER UP!
DINGHY SECURITY

Y our Power Cat will have powered davits that allow the dinghy to be hoisted out of the water and secured. Bigger cats might have a platform that gets lowered into the water and the dinghy rested upon it and then raised up level to the deck.

PC with Dinghy Platform in raised position

Most, though, are raised by lines that attach to U-bolts fitted to the hull of the dinghy—or to bridles that are attached to a set of U-bolts. Why use davits? These are the two primary reasons:

Security: For various reasons—largely economic, but some just for the pleasure of the thing (joyriding kids, perhaps)—your RIB-type dinghy with its 10-15 HP outboard makes a tempting object for thieves. Mostly down-island, but not only there—the rich Virgin Islands have their opportunistic thieves as well as the less prosperous Grenadines, St. Lucia, and Dominica. St. Martin's Grand Case or Marigot bays will sometimes serve as a source of personal transport for Anguillans who have missed the last ferry.

So, if you're chartering in one of these islands, the briefers at the base will alert you to the risks and guide you on safeguarding your vessel.

There are two main security scenarios—when the dinghy is attached to the mothership whilst all aboard are sleeping, or when the dinghy is at the dock while the crew is cavorting—sorry, we mean dining sedately ashore. On the dock, where there are many watching eyes, a basic lock and cable will do—you are really only trying to make your dinghy less attractive a target than the unlocked one parked right next to it.

WHEN ALL IS quiet in the mooring field and everyone is asleep, using the charter-company supplied wire and padlock often will be insufficient deterrence—the wire alone will not put off experienced thieves. Most will carry a cutter that'll nip through wire before you can say, "Where's the dinghy?" In these places, the charter company will show you how to lift your dink up at night before you turn in. If it does disappear and it wasn't secured as we describe, your insurance coverage will probably be useless. Raise it up!

AND WHEN AT anchor or on a mooring you might be tempted to leave the dinghy in the water. There's always a reason--you might need it first thing in the morning or it's in the way of the BBQ grill. Or, as many charters do, you might have rented a second dinghy so the younger members of the group can go diving while the olds go beach combing.

If that is the case, make sure it is well secured to the mothership by strong cables and locks. A big dinghy may be worth $25,000 or more and they are much in demand—or their engines are—in many parts of the Caribbean.

So, raise it or lock it up. Better still, do both.

25

PLUG 'N' PLAY
POWER POINTS

The electrical conveniences made possible by the generator on modern boats have made massive and welcome improvements to the quality of life aboard ship. Aircon! Microwave! Big-Screen Video! Watermaker! Underwater Lighting! All amazing.

And the increases in power requirements for the old familiar chart plotters, ice makers, and other devices have made the genset the go-to source for battery charging, too. But often these sophisticated displays and devices are treated with a casual disregard rather than the molly-coddling they deserve—and, frankly, require.

Marine electronics are just as sensitive as those you have at home. You wouldn't dream of simply pulling the plug on your appliances lest you destroy the careful programming you've entered. Same with that chartplotter for instance: it's a computer, with sensitivities to match. Ditto with the other navigation instruments, air conditioning units, refrigeration, and entertainment equipment. Plus, they live near salt water, and other indignities such as spilled drinks, slimy guacamole, sticky sunscreen, and the like.

When first boarding the charter yacht, or when receiving the Boat Briefing, look in the chart table or under the seat nearby for a copy of the electronics manuals. Spend a few minutes learning the basics of how the chartplotter, the VHF and the Bluetooth stereo operate. If the manual has been removed or can't be found, you can easily look the model up on the internet.

You need to know not just how to properly start them up but how to manage the waypoints and routes that have most likely been installed by previous operators. Disregard all waypoints and routes since you can't be sure of their accuracy—delete them if you have time. Learn the proper procedure for powering up all instruments. When it comes to powering-down these devices, remember to turn off the individual power buttons at each instrument at the helm station. Don't just kill the breaker at the electrical panel.

Equally important, if you're on a boat with a generator, the air conditioning units should be turned off at the individual cabin controls before disconnecting from shore power. The reason to turn them on and off individually in each cabin—and not just via the main breaker—is this: if left on when the shore power is disconnected at the box or the genset abruptly turned off, there is a real danger of a system overload when the electrical supply is reinstated.

When the generator is next fired up and the aircon breaker flipped on there's such a huge current draw as 4-6 aircon units try to start at the same time that the generator will likely shut itself down in protest. They need to be powered up one-by-one with a 5-10 minute delay between each.

This air conditioning capability is the big game-changing application on modern cruising yachts. The distribution of the chilled air differs from one model to the next, but may be divided into three zones—Port and Starboard hulls and the Saloon, for example on the typical four cabin cat, where the temperature of the two cabins in each hull is identical. When there are more cabins or an atypical layout, there may be zones for each cabin—meaning that the occupants of each cabin choose their own temperature.

The reality of onboard air conditioning, however, is that it is not easy to maintain a temperature. Cold air sinks into the two hulls and the saloon and galley have large 'windows' that let in tropical sunshine. it's often bone-chillingly cold or barely cool. Make sure you get plenty of blankets at the start of the journey to compensate for the chill.

> **NOTE**: *In the saloon and your cabins, keep closed the sun-shields under your hatches and the blinds covering the windows/portlights to prevent them becoming greenhouses when the sun is shining. It'll be a lot easier and quicker for the genset to cool them down at the end of the day.*

So, don't unplug your boat from shore power without first powering down all the heavy energy consumers on your boat, starting with all the aircon units at the individual saloon and cabin controls and then all the 110/220 volt aircon and battery charger breakers at the nav. station followed by turning off the 110/220 volt AC input breaker or change-over gate. Only then unplug from the power post—after turning that off, too, since you don't want any risk of a current arc.

STATE OF CHARGE: During your first 24 hours aboard, pay special attention to electrical consumption as displayed at what's called the distribution or breaker panel. Not all battery systems on charter yachts are maintained to perfection, so you'll need to make sure your batteries hold sufficient charge to chill the refrigerators overnight if the generator isn't running.

> **Note**: *A fully charged 12-volt battery system should be taken to a level of 14.2-14.4 volts initially, if there is no drain on the system. Once the charger is disconnected, the voltage should fall to around 12.8 volts. If the batteries don't reach that level after hours of charging, or if they rapidly lose their charge, you may have problems.*

As part of the daily routine, check the status of the batteries from the saloon distribution panel. If the house voltage is below 12v, you'll need to run an engine or the generator to charge up again if you want things to keep working.

And be aware that the recommendation for most charter yachts is that the generator not be running whilst the vessel is underway, since the water intake for the genny is close to the surface and can easily suck in air, seaweed, and other substances—and quickly run dry and overheat as the boat rolls in swell. Clearing that mess is a big job and best avoided by not incurring the problem in the first place.

DAILY PRACTICE
CHECKS AND BALANCES

W **OPILG**

Water Out, People In, Look Good

Water Out:

Close port lights and hatches and dog (latch) them tight.

Pump bilges using the 'manual' feature of the electric bilge pump switch. Flick it back to 'auto' afterward.

People In:

Remind everyone it's a boat, not a holiday cottage.

"One hand for me and one for the ship."

Close all the gates at the side and back of the boat.

Look Good:

Flags flying smartly

Laundry off the lifelines.

Swim ladder up.

All doors, lockers, drawers, fridges, oven doors, secured from slamming about when rolling through a ferry wake or adverse sea conditions underway.

WOBBLE (ENGINE AND GENERATOR CHECKS)

WATER: Check the coolant levels. Check water strainer for debris. Watch for sea grass or even jelly fish in the basket! If you do need to clean it out, first close the seacock (valve) leading to it from the inside of the hull. Don't forget to reopen it afterward! And, if clearing jelly fish, place your hand in a plastic bag or kitchen gloves first to avoid stings.

OIL LEVELS: Check the dipstick for quantity and color.

BELTS: Check tightness and degree of wear. (If the belt is accessible —most turbo diesels have semi- or fully enclosed belt drives.)

BILGE: look beneath the engine for oil or coolant leaks.

LOOKAROUND: Check all round the engine compartment for loose hose clamps, filler caps accidentally not replaced by last technician, nuts and bolts etc. Examine all electrical connections for signs of overheating. If anything is amiss, it'll show some evidence.

. . .

EXHAUST: Once you've exited the engine compartment, fire up the engines and genset and look over the side for water gushing out in spurts. If it's not, close down that engine and check that the seacock leading to the strainer is open. If it is open you may have an issue—so check the strainer basket for seagrass or weed. If it's clear, call the base for assistance.

LOCK, LASH AND SECURE

When preparing for departure, look around above and below decks, checking for weak points in these areas:

Hatches and ports: The hatches and opening portlights (aka 'windows') should already be closed but now's the time to double-check that they've been closed securely. Pay extra attention to the more common Lewmar hatches, which can be locked on a half-latch that looks secure but which is not watertight (it's designed to allow some ventilation whilst keeping vertically falling rain out).

DOORS, DRAWERS, LOCKERS, AND CABINETS: These should already be locked if you're underway. Before a squall hits, make sure that doors and drawers can't fly open, throwing their contents into the boat or at whoever may be down below. Pay special attention to drawers with knives, and lockers containing glass jars and wine bottles. You do not want to be cleaning up spilled olive oil, soy sauce, and ketchup in a rolling boat.

Keep everything secure!

HEADS AND TOILETS: Drain all toilet bowls of as much water as possible and lower the lid—objects can fall into the bowl easily in bouncy seas. Drain the shower sump, too, since there are often a few cups of gray water sluicing around. Secure toothbrushes, shampoo, and glass items, towels and anything that might fall and get wet or break.

BREAKER/DISTRIBUTION Panel: Turn off power to all units that don't need to be on. Lights, fans, and air conditioning units—and any other extraneous electrical equipment. Do leave the bilge pumps powered on in 'auto' mode, though, since the movement will send trapped water sloshing about the bilges to trip the float switches.

27

SICK DAZE
FEELIN' WOOZY

Nothing will impact your happiness aboard the yacht as much as a case of seasickness. Not only your happiness, should you be the one suffering, but the happiness of those around you. If you know or suspect that you or anyone aboard is susceptible, then you should take adequate preventative action. Focusing your eyes on close objects is known to set vulnerable people off. So, unless you're sure you can handle it, put down that book (until safely at anchor or on a mooring). Turn off those handheld devices (likewise).

There are a number of medications available for seasickness but they each have their complications. Many of these remedies will induce drowsiness, lethargy, dry mouth, and other symptoms. The most important part of taking these meds is to take them early. Most are for prevention of sea-sickness, not its cure. If you feel symptoms, it is often too late to do anything.

THE MOST EFFECTIVE drug seems to be the *Scopolamine* trans-dermal patch. Talk to your doctor first—there may be side effects that won't help your situation. For most people though, this is amazingly effective and has minimal side effects. Every other remedy pales in comparison.

THE OTHER COMMON medication is *Stugeron*—which has not gone through the expensive process of getting approval from the US Food and Drug Administration but has been widely accepted in Europe, the UK, and elsewhere. You may be able to buy it over the counter in many island pharmacies especially those that either are or were UK or French/Dutch territories..

FOR THOSE WITH occasionally mild reactions, ginger can work wonders. Crystallized ginger is good or ginger in various candy or chewable forms. Straight ginger root is good, too—grate some fresh ginger into soda water or add the ginger to a cup of tea. Some of the fizzy soft drinks like the local ginger beer can be a good stomach settler—but make sure your choice contains actual ginger and not just a ginger flavoring.

DUTY REQUIRES we point out that sea-sickness is associated with hangovers and alcohol—it might be best to refrain from excessive indulgence! One side effect of drinking alcohol, of course, is dehydration. Stay hydrated.

If a member of your party does come down with the Queazies, get them into the water when you're anchored or moored. A lot of the problem lies in the confusion induced by the rapid movements in all three dimensions as the yacht is rocked by swell and wind. If you are able to stop in a cove and get the crew swimming, the mood generally improves immensely.

If all else fails, ease the ailing mariner into the shade of a palm tree and let them regain their equilibrium—minus the Painkiller.

In Conclusion: The world of bareboat charters is wide and welcoming. There's a place for every taste—from hardcore sailor to laid-back relaxaholic. Some people want to cram in as much action as the day will accommodate while others want to do as little as possible other than cruise from one beach to the next and snooze in the shade. Most are somewhere in the middle.

No MATTER which category you see yourself in, the same rules apply for everyone:

•Be Careful.

•Be Patient.

•Plan your day.

•Know your boat.

•Know the local regulations.

•Be considerate of other cruisers.

•Clean up after yourself.

•Give yourself time.

•Have fun.

•And remember our mantra: *Easy Does It.*

28

LINKS and QR CODES

Here is a link to our website and the pages containing the many other links and references for different Caribbean destinations and varied sources of information:

https://tinyurl.com/4m6263nm

AND IF YOU have any questions or comments related to the material in this book, please get in touch at

info@smartercharterguides.com

NOTE: *(If direct links are not operable). We are using QR codes to point directly to the services mentioned by way of a smartphone or tablet. If you are unfamiliar with their use, check online—iPhones are equipped to read the codes directly from the camera app, while Android and other devices might require a free app from the Play store (we like 'QR Scanner' by Trend Micro).*

QR11

Virgin Islands Guide

Good Moon Farm
BVI

SmarterCharter
Safety Packet

Windguru (BVI)

Deb Mahan
Meal Plan

SmarterCharter
Links Pages

QR12

Carib Security Index   Traveltalk Online

VI Search Rescue   Noonsite

Carib Sailing Coach   Doyle Guides

Acknowledgments

The authors wish to thank the hundreds of students, clients, and colleagues who have been the catalysts for this project. Without their questions, comments, and enthusiastic commitment to the art and science of cruising under sail, we wouldn't have started the conversa-tion that led us down this path.

We would also like to thank the management and ownership of the many charter companies who have encouraged us in putting these books together.

Special thanks to Kim Downing for the excellent illustrations.

A NOTE ON THE AUTHORS:

Neither of us started out in a maritime school. While we may have put together a number of instructor credentials and professional qualifications, our boating was mostly learned piecemeal—some from friends, from dads, some from Scouts, some from friends, and a good deal from racing. Much of this was of great value and some—such as racing—less so.

We've been cruising Caribbean waters for decades, in many capacities—from sailing instructor to charter company owner, corporate manager, and professional coach. Between us we've seen it all and done most of it. We've made mistakes, dragged anchor, snagged propellers, bounced off docks and off the seabed—so we know what we are talking about. "If you haven't been aground, you haven't been around," they say. Well, we've been around.

Michael Domican (l), David Blacklock (r)

We would love to hear from you!

Here's how to reach us:

Drop us a line at: info@smartercharterguides.com

Facebook: https://www.facebook.com/CharterGuides/

On the Web: https://www.smartercharterguides.com/

Credit Dept.

The authors wish to thank the hundreds of students, clients, and colleagues who have been the catalysts for this project. Without their questions, comments, and enthusiastic commitment to the art and science of bareboat cruising, we wouldn't have started the conversations that led us down this path.

We would also like to thank the management and crews of the many charter companies who have encouraged us in putting these books together.

Photography:

COVER: Photographer: Jerome Kelagopian/The Moorings

Interior photography: Michael Domican/David Blacklock /Andrew Lewis/ Jerome Kelagopian

Special thanks to Kim Downing for the excellent illustrations.

Made in United States
North Haven, CT
11 October 2022

25270797R00104